Knowledge, Freedom, and Taste

Kant Studien Supplementa

On behalf of the Kant-Gesellschaft
edited by
Manfred Baum, Bernd Dörflinger,
Heiner F. Klemme and Konstantin Pollok

Volume 1

Knowledge, Freedom, and Taste

Internationaler Kant-Preis 2024: Paul Guyer

Edited by
Konstantin Pollok

DE GRUYTER

ISBN 978-3-11-154389-5
e-ISBN (PDF) 978-3-11-154473-1
e-ISBN (EPUB) 978-3-11-154542-4
ISSN 2510-9596
DOI https://doi.org/10.1515/9783111544731

This work is licensed under the Creative Commons Attribution 4.0 International License.
For details go to https://creativecommons.org/licenses/by/4.0/.

Creative Commons license terms for re-use do not apply to any content that is not part of the Open Access publication (such as graphs, figures, photos, excerpts, etc.). These may require obtaining further permission from the rights holder. The obligation to research and clear permission lies solely with the party re-using the material.

Library of Congress Control Number: 2024941603

Bibliographic information published by the Deutsche Nationalbibliothek
The Deutsche Nationalbibliothek lists this publication in the Deutsche Nationalbibliografie; detailed bibliographic data are available on the Internet at http://dnb.dnb.de.

© 2024 the author(s), published by Walter de Gruyter GmbH, Berlin/Boston.
This book is published open access at www.degruyter.com.
Printing and binding: CPI books GmbH, Leck

www.degruyter.com

Das letzte bekannte Bildnis Immanuel Kants zu seinen Lebzeiten. Zeichnung – „[Friedrich Heinrich Leopold] Baltruschatis fecit" – und Kants Eintrag — „Ad poenitendum properat, cito qui iudicat. I Kant. d. 16 Ianuarii 1802." — in das Stammbuch von „C. H. B.", einem Studenten der Albertus-Universität Königsberg, das dieser in den Jahren 1802 bis 1812 geführt hat. – Autographensammlung der Universitätsbibliothek, Johannes Gutenberg-Universität Mainz, Manuskript, Signatur 171, S. 25. – Vgl. Richter, Günter; Malter, Rudolf: „Das Stammbuch C. H. B. 1802(–12) mit einem Eintrag Immanuel Kants". In: *Kant-Studien* 72/2 (1981), 161–69.

Contents

List of Abbreviations —— IX

Konstantin Pollok
Editorial —— 1

Frederick Rauscher
Guyer on Empirical and Transcendental Grounds for Morality —— 3

Lucas Thorpe
Guyer, Sellars and Kant on the Dignity and Value of Freedom —— 21

Julian Wuerth
Guyer, the Grounding of Kant's Categorical Imperative, and the Elimination of Sensibility Procedure —— 39

Kate Moran
A Modest Defense of the Personal Highest Good —— 57

Wiebke Deimling
The Passion for Freedom and the Passion for the Ultimate Means —— 77

Reed Winegar
The Beautiful and the Sublime in Kant's Early Natural Philosophy —— 95

Paul Guyer
Response —— 117

Notes on Authors —— 137

List of Abbreviations

Citations of Kant's works refer to the Akademie-Ausgabe:
Kant's gesammelte Schriften, 29 vols., vol. 1–22 ed. by Königlich Preussische Akademie der Wissenschaften, vol. 23 ed. by Deutsche Akademie der Wissenschaften zu Berlin, vols. 24– ed. by Akademie der Wissenschaften zu Göttingen, Berlin: Walter de Gruyter, 1900–.

Unless otherwise noted, authors use translations from *The Cambridge Edition of the Works of Immanuel Kant*, ed. by Paul Guyer and Allen W. Wood, Cambridge/New York: Cambridge University Press, 1992–).

Abbreviations used within citations include the following:

AA	Akademie-Ausgabe
Anth	Anthropologie in pragmatischer Hinsicht (AA 07)
BDG	Der einzig mögliche Beweisgrund zu einer Demonstration des Daseins Gottes (AA 02)
BGSE	Beobachtungen über das Gefühl des Schönen und Erhabenen (AA 02)
Br	Briefe (AA 10-13)
GMS	Grundlegung zur Metaphysik der Sitten (AA 04)
IaG	Idee zu einer allgemeinen Geschichte in weltbürgerlicher Absicht (AA 08)
KpV	Kritik der praktischen Vernunft (AA 05)
KrV	Kritik der reinen Vernunft (zu zitieren nach Originalpaginierung A/B)
KU	Kritik der Urteilskraft (AA 05)
MS	Die Metaphysik der Sitten (AA 06)
NTH	Allgemeine Naturgeschichte und Theorie des Himmels oder Versuch von der Verfassung und dem mechanischen Ursprunge des ganzen Weltgebäudes nach Newtonischen Grundsätzen abgehandelt (AA 01)
RGV	Die Religion innerhalb der Grenzen der bloßen Vernunft (AA 06)
Refl	Reflexionen (AA 14-19)
UD	Untersuchung über die Deutlichkeit der Grundsätze der natürlichen Theologie und der Moral (AA 02) [Inquiry Concerning the Distinctness of the Principles of Natural Theology and Morality]

V-Anth/Busolt	Vorlesungen Wintersemester 1788/1789 Busolt (AA 25)
V-Anth/Collins	Vorlesungen Wintersemester 1772/1773 Collins (AA 25)
V-Anth/Mensch	Vorlesungen Wintersemester 1781/1782 Menschenkunde, Petersburg (AA 25)
V-Anth/Mron	Vorlesungen Wintersemester 1784/1785 Mrongovius (AA 25
V-Mo/Collins	Vorlesungen Wintersemester 1784/1785 Moralphilosophie Collins (AA 27)
V-Mo/Mron	Moral Mrongovius (Grundl.: 1774/75 bzw. 76/77) (AA 27)
V-Mo/Mron II	Vorlesungen Wintersemester 1784/1785 Moral Mrongovius II (AA 29)
V-NR/Feyerabend	Naturrecht Feyerabend (Winter 1784) (AA 27)
V-PP/Herder	Praktische Philosophie Herder (1763/64 bzw. 64/65) (AA 27)

Konstantin Pollok
Editorial

Das Jubiläum von Kants 300. Geburtstag markiert den Beginn der *Kant-Studien Supplementa*. Es bestätigt Hans Vaihingers 1897 im ersten Heft der *Kant-Studien* geäußerte Vermutung, „die Philosophie [...] stehe noch immer, und voraussichtlich noch auf lange Zeit hinaus, unter dem Zeichen Kants."[1] Diese neue Reihe der *Kant-Studien Supplementa* wird zusätzlich zu den *Kant-Studien* und der seit 1906 bestehenden Reihe der *Kant-Studien Ergänzungshefte* erscheinen. Während letztere Monographien und Sammelbände zur Philosophie Kants umfasst, verdanken die Supplementa ihre Idee der Institution des Internationalen Kant-Preises.

Seit 1965 veranstaltet die Kant-Gesellschaft in Zusammenarbeit mit lokalen Kant-Forscher*innen in der Regel im Abstand von fünf Jahren den „Internationalen Kant-Kongress". Seit 2000 wird auf diesem „Internationalen Kant-Kongress" jeweils ein „Internationaler Kant-Preis" an eine herausragende Persönlichkeit verliehen, die sich nachhaltig um die Philosophie Kants verdient gemacht hat. Die bisherigen Preisträger*innen sind: Peter F. Strawson (2000), Dieter Henrich (2004), Henry E. Allison (2005), Mario Caimi (2010), Onora O'Neill (2015) und Gerold Prauss (2019). Diese Auszeichnungen wurden durch die großzügige Finanzierung der ZEIT-Stiftung Ebelin und Gerd Bucerius (bis 2005) sowie der Fritz Thyssen Stiftung (seit 2010) ermöglicht.

Um diesem „Internationalen Kant-Preis" etwas mehr philosophische Substanz zu verleihen, als dies in einer Laudatio bei der Preisverleihung möglich ist, werden im Jubiläumsjahr 2024 die *Kant-Studien Supplementa* ins Leben gerufen. Ihr Ziel ist zum einen die Würdigung und philosophische Auseinandersetzung mit dem Lebenswerk des Preisträgers bzw. der Preisträgerin. Zum anderen demonstriert die Auswahl der Autor*innen der *Kant-Studien Supplementa*, dass nicht nur das Werk, sondern auch die Person des Preisträgers bzw. der Preisträgerin als akademische Lehrkraft preiswürdig ist. Denn die *Kant-Studien Supplementa* enthalten Originalbeiträge von Kant-Forscher*innen, die unter der Leitung des Preisträgers bzw. der Preisträgerin studiert und eventuell sogar promoviert haben, und deren eigene Philosophie deshalb maßgeblich von der Auseinandersetzung mit der Forschung des Preisträgers bzw. der Preisträgerin geprägt ist. Abgerundet wird das Heft jeweils mit einer Replik des Preisträgers bzw. der Preisträgerin auf diese Beiträge.

Sowohl das Thema des 14. Internationalen Kant-Kongresses 2024 – Kants Projekt der Aufklärung – im Gedenken an den 300. Geburtstag Kants und im Hinblick

---

1 Vaihinger, Hans: „Zur Einführung". In: *Kant-Studien*. Band 1, Heft 1, 1897, 1–8, hier 1.

Open Access. © 2024 the author(s), published by De Gruyter. This work is licensed under the Creative Commons Attribution 4.0 International License.
https://doi.org/10.1515/9783111544731-001

auf die politischen Entwicklungen unserer Tage, als auch der diesjährige Kant-Preisträger Paul Guyer und der Kreis seiner Schüler*innen bekräftigen für die *Kant-Studien Supplementa*, was Vaihinger bereits 1897 programmatisch für die *Kant-Studien* vorgegeben hat: „Und da Kants Philosophie ein Gemeingut aller Kulturnationen geworden ist, da seine Werke, seine Begriffe, seine Ideen nicht blos in Deutschland, sondern in demselben Masse auch im Ausland wirksame Mächte geworden sind, so musste dies Organ einen internationalen Charakter annehmen."[2] In diesem Sinne tragen die *Kant-Studien Supplementa* dazu bei, dass *Kants Projekt der Aufklärung* auch weiterhin ein kosmopolitisches Projekt bleibt.

Mainz, im Mai 2024

---

2 Vaihinger, „Zur Einführung", 5.

Frederick Rauscher
Guyer on Empirical and Transcendental Grounds for Morality

Abstract: Paul Guyer has been reluctant to accept any ontological claims about persons in themselves as a basis for morality, preferring when possible empirical explanations of freedom of the will or its value. While he recognizes the limitations of empirical grounds, he also strives to avoid transcendental grounds, equating them with ontological claims about transcendent reality. I review the reasoning that Guyer has given over his career for these claims and suggest that one large reason for his hesitation is that his interpretation puts too much weight on a transcendental freedom of the will and not enough on a transcendental freedom of reason, particularly in *Groundwork* III. Kant can use this status of reason to provide a transcendental ground for the moral law as a causal law for our empirical will and to be a source of moral value without invoking the heavy ontology that Guyer wishes Kant had avoided.

Keywords: reason, will, transcendental, empirical, naturalism

"We may now not be much tempted by Kant's transcendental realism, but then again we may not be much tempted by his transcendental idealism" says Paul Guyer after concluding that Kant's moral theory rests on a claim to the transcendental reality of freedom.[1] One wonders whether the problem is neither the realism nor the idealism but the *transcendental* aspect of this temptation. Guyer has, of course, been highly critical of Kant's transcendental idealism as an ontological claim that objects in themselves can be known to be non-spatial and non-temporal, from *Kant and the Claims of Knowledge* in 1987 to "Transcendental Idealism: What and Why" in 2017.[2] He has more generally resisted Kant's arguments that we can make legitimate claims about things in themselves, including claims about the kinds of beings that we humans are in ourselves. This objection to Kant's ontology is really an objection to Kant's claims about objects that transcend our empirical grasp. In ethics this has led Guyer to argue that Kant had an empirical basis for moral claims about the value and actuality of freedom early in his philosophical

---

[1] Guyer, Paul, *Kant on the Rationality of Morality*, Cambridge 2019, 65.
[2] Guyer, Paul, *Kant and the Claims of Knowledge*, Cambridge 1987. Guyer, Paul, "Transcendental Idealism: What and Why?", in *The Palgrave Kant Handbook*, ed. by M. Altman. London 2017, 71–90.

career that continued in some strands of his thought. More recently he has modified those claims to allow, with some regret as in the passage just quoted, that Kant's ethics must be grounded in non-empirical claims.

I will argue here that Guyer's preference for empirical grounds for Kant's ethics is misplaced, and that further, Kant does not require as much of the ontology that Guyer finds hard to swallow as Guyer supposes. The discussion will focus on two aspects of Kant's ethics that Guyer discusses in empirical terms — the value of freedom and the fact of freedom — and will show that in both cases they are dependent upon reason in a way that avoids much of the transcendent claims about them that so worries Guyer.

Much of the core discussion hinges on different approaches to interpreting *Groundwork* III, which Guyer takes to contain Kant's core transcendental argument to justify morality. Over the past decades, Guyer's interpretation of *Groundwork* III has shifted in emphasis although the core understanding of Kant's argument has remained the same. I will look at *Groundwork* III in more detail later in this paper, after setting the stage by showing how Guyer frames the expectations for Kant's *Groundwork* III argument.

1 On Freedom as the Highest Value

Guyer has repeatedly emphasized Kant's identification of freedom as the central value in morality. He has repeatedly quoted from passages such as this one from Kant's Mrongovius Lectures on Ethics

> if all creatures had a faculty of choice bound to sensuous desires, the world would have no value; the inner value of the world, the *summum bonum*, is the freedom to act in accordance with a faculty of choice that is not necessitated. Freedom is therefore the inner value of the world. (V-Mo/Mron, AA 27: 1482).

But *why* is freedom valuable? Guyer would prefer Kant to have based the value of freedom on empirical grounds. His paper "Naturalistic and Transcendental Moments in Kant's Moral Philosophy"[3] draws largely on Kant's notes in his own copy of *Observations on the Feeling of the Beautiful and Sublime* and other notes in some of his textbooks to show that Kant considered an argument for the moral law based on the empirical fact that human beings value their own freedom. Guyer calls this

---

[3] Guyer, Paul, "Naturalistic and Transcendental Moments in Kant's Moral Philosophy", *Inquiry* 50, 2007, 444–464.

"Kant's original naturalistic ethics".[4] Here, as shown in some of those notes,[5] Kant states that human beings have a natural desire to avoid being dominated by others and as well as a feeling of satisfaction in life linked to consciousness of freedom. The value of freedom is thus a psychological fact about human beings and is not dependent upon any metaphysical claim to a non-natural freedom, nor is it universally attributed to rational beings but is limited to actual human beings and their particular nature. Reason does play a role in relation to freedom: rules from reason provide a way to regulate our freedom to avoid problems if free actions themselves undermine the possibility of performing other future free actions. Guyer sees Kant here as offering an early version of the categorical imperative as a rule to ensure the maximal extent of freedom not only for oneself but also for other free beings. Guyer concedes that Kant does not have the resources here to include the freedom of others in this kind of calculation and can really only make a conclusion regarding a pragmatic rule to guarantee one's own maximally consistent freedom.[6]

Guyer sees Kant as continuing to assert the value of freedom in his course lectures up through the 1780s by tying it to the feeling of life. As Guyer concedes, Kant also takes freedom to be a mixed blessing in these lectures. Freedom is "the inner worth of the world" yet "the most terrible thing there can be" if it is not restrained by laws (V-Mo/Collins, AA 27: 344). Reason must provide a rule to rein in freedom. At this point, one might wonder why freedom is so valuable if it can also be a terrible thing. How can something valuable include instances in practice in which it is not valuable? This apparent paradox dissolves, however, when one sees the particular acts that Kant considers terrible. Some free acts have as their effect the destruction or prevention of other free acts. A use of freedom that effectively destroys a persons' capacity for freedom is terrible because it "minimizes rather than maximizes his freedom over what should have been a multitude of possibilities for action", as Guyer explains.[7] Thus freedom can still be a value based in some way empirically, but the maximization of that value requires a consistency of application that only the guidance of reason can provide.

---

4 Guyer, "Naturalistic", 445.
5 Henry Allison points out in his reply to Guyer's article that Kant offered many other contrasting claims in these notes, so that the mere presence of some claims in a few isolated notes is not enough evidence to claim that the view was Kant's considered view at the time. This point is well taken but does not show that at least some of the time Kant was at least toying with these ideas. The value of Kant's unpublished notes is precisely that we are able to see Kant working through various ideas before settling on a version to publish. See Henry Allison, "Comments on Guyer", *Inquiry* 50, 2007, 480–488.
6 Guyer, "Naturalistic", 449–450.
7 Guyer, "Naturalistic", 450.

The value of freedom and empirical support for that claim is the position Guyer sees primarily in Kant's course lectures and his own notes for those lectures. As Guyer himself says, his interpretation of freedom as the central value "is based on the assumption that he revealed its premise most clearly in lectures".[8] But this alone is insufficient evidence that Kant actually thought that freedom was the central value, let alone that it did not require any non-empirical basis. Kant's lack of discussion in his ethics and natural right lectures of a metaphysical or transcendental basis for freedom, and the deeper discussion of morality that places freedom in a transcendental context, may simply stem from the fact that these lectures were geared toward students who Kant may have thought incapable of comprehending the difficult proofs along the lines of *Groundwork* III. In an analogous way Kant does not present his transcendental deduction of the categories in his metaphysics lectures. Perhaps the fact that Kant reserved his deepest transcendental discussion of the role of freedom in morality to the second *Critique* and the *Groundwork* speaks more to its importance than its unimportance in Kant's system.

The judgment Guyer ultimately makes about Kant's empirical discussion of the value of freedom, and thus of its role as a foundation for morality, is well put in this passage from Guyer's survey book *Kant*:

> It is not clear that such a [psychological empirical] foundation for morality would be consistent with Kant's insistence that the moral law must be valid for every rational being, human or otherwise, thus that "a pure moral philosophy" must be "completely cleansed of everything that may be only empirical and that belongs to anthropology" (G, 4:389). But it is also not clear whether Kant really has an alternative but equally gripping account of the normative force of the moral law, so this psychological assumption may play an indispensable role in Kant's subsequent moral philosophy even if he does not acknowledge it.[9]

Thus, while Guyer recognizes the limits that an empirical foundation for morality might have, he is skeptical that Kant can provide any transcendental replacement that would prove the value of freedom.

Allowing that Kant did offer at least some empirical support for the value of freedom at least in the pre-critical period, he certainly moved to a transcendental approach in the critical period. Guyer says that Kant rarely tries to give a transcendental defense of the value of freedom, discussing this issue only in the *Groundwork*. In other places Kant does not require a proof of a metaphysical fact of freedom but either rests on the empirical invocation of the practical value or an

---

8 Guyer, Paul, *Virtues of Freedom*, Oxford 2016, vi–vii.
9 Guyer, Paul, *Kant*, New York 2006, 179.

assumption that humans do value freedom.[10] As Guyer sees it in the paper "Naturalistic and Transcendental Approaches", Kant moves from this early naturalistic, empirical defense of the value of freedom to a simple assertion of the value of freedom in the first sections of the *Groundwork*.[11] Had Kant rested there, he could still be said to have offered a sound moral theory in the argument that the categorical imperative is the means by which we can realize that freedom. But, Guyer laments, Kant does not rest there. Kant instead plows ahead to offer a transcendental argument in *Groundwork* III for the value of freedom based upon an attempted proof that we human beings are in fact rational beings who are necessarily subject to the categorical imperative.[12] And, worse, the argument provided "actually sidesteps the normative task of motivating the premise of the absolute value of freedom", that is, it does not succeed in providing nor even aim at a defense of the value of freedom.[13] This argument will be examined later, but at this point it is important to note that Guyer attributes to Kant a gap in his overall defense of morality — namely the need for a non-empirical ground for the value of freedom that would replace the earlier empirical, psychological ground for the value of freedom — that Kant then fails to fill despite his immense effort in *Groundwork* III. I will suggest later that Kant did not intend *Groundwork* III to play this role at all, and that Kant did not see the value of freedom as a self-standing ground for morality but as itself a value dependent upon reason itself.

Before jumping into an assessment of *Groundwork* III, there is a larger concern regarding Guyer's preference for an empirical support for the value of freedom. Empirical bases are one and all contingent. While love of freedom and recognition of the personal benefits of freedom may be widespread, if not universal, in modern liberal democratic society, they are only contingently so. Freedom has certainly not been the highest value of individuals throughout history and cultures but rests upon particular self-conceptions in human cultures; religious values and dedication to other kinds of causes deemed to have more importance than individual autonomy are frequent in history and around the world. When Guyer admits that Kant's early exploration of an empirical basis for morality is insufficient, Guyer stresses that it lacks universality: one can have a psychological reason to value one's own freedom as essential for one's own fulfillment, but one does not have any similar reason to value the freedom of others. Guyer does not stress its lack of necessity: even if every human being did value their own freedom, and even if (contra Kant's

---

10 Guyer, *Virtues*, v–vi.
11 Guyer, "Naturalistic", 451.
12 Guyer, "Naturalistic", 449–450.
13 Guyer, "Naturalistic", 452.

and Guyer's allowances) every human being also valued the freedom of others, such universal agreement would fail to possess the necessity that must accompany morality. As Kant says in the Preface to the *Groundwork* "Everyone must grant that a law, if it is to hold morally, that is, as a ground of an obligation, must carry with it absolute necessity" (GMS, AA 04: 389). Kant's immediate move in the Preface is to claim that the required necessary "ground of obligation here must [...] be sought [...] a priori simply in concepts of pure reason" and that "any other precept which is based on principles of mere experience — even if it is universal in a certain respect" can never be a moral law. Thus Kant's rejection of an empirical basis for morality is based in part upon the need for the kind of necessity that can stem only from pure reason. If we are to find any value to act as a ground of obligation, we are not going to find it empirically but only in pure reason.

Guyer, of course, recognizes that Kant hopes for universality and necessity rather than generality and contingency, but takes Kant to fail in the quest for that ground for morality. A presented in the paper "Naturalistic and Transcendental", the cause is a failure on Kant's part to prove that freedom has a value through what Guyer sees as Kant's attempted transcendental argument in *Groundwork* III to prove that human beings are obligated to follow the categorical imperative. Rather than trying to prove through transcendental argument that freedom has a value, Kant's goal in *Groundwork* III is to prove that we human beings as things in ourselves are rational beings, and as rational beings are subject to the moral law.[14] Kant, Guyer holds here, offers no normative grounds to argue for the value of freedom and thus no normative grounds to argue that we ought to follow the categorical imperative because it promotes the value of freedom, instead only claiming that as noumenal things in ourselves we are really free, rational beings obligated to follow the moral law.[15] (As mentioned earlier, I will examine the details of *Groundwork* III below).

Guyer has changed his mind about this overall claim[16] and now rejects the view that Kant ever intended to prove the value of freedom directly through any

---

14 Guyer, "Naturalistic", 455.
15 Guyer, "Naturalistic", 459.
16 One of the virtues of Guyer's work on Kant is his openness to changing his interpretations in light of other analysis by himself or others. In this he does not emulate Kant, who never seems to have admitted to changing any view throughout his career. Regarding *Groundwork* III, the change I will describe above is not Guyer's only change of interpretation. In the "Naturalistic and Transcendental" paper, Guyer admits to having altered his interpretation of the aim of Kant's argument; in some earlier papers Guyer had taken Kant to be trying to prove that human beings always act freely, but he had rejected that view and at the time of "Naturalistic and Transcendental" he had seen Kant as first attempting to prove that we are obligated to the categorical imperative, and only then to conclude that we are free to act ("Naturalistic", 463, fn. 21, referencing Guyer, "Self-

transcendental argument. He now holds that Kant intended to derive moral value from an application of pure reason to a fact about human beings, namely, the fact that we are free. Since that fact is supposed to be the target of Kant's transcendental argument in *Groundwork* III, my discussion of that issue will examine Guyer's claims about the specific structure of Kant's argument in *Groundwork* III. Guyer is equally suspicious of transcendental claims about freedom as a capacity as he was suspicious of transcendental claims regarding the value of freedom.

Before turning to that section, allow me to summarize a few important claims regarding the value of freedom. First, Guyer takes the value of freedom to lie at the heart of morality and right; it is not derived from anything else. The basis is either empirical — which as we saw would lack necessity even if it had universality based on human nature — or transcendental. Guyer sees Kant as moving toward a transcendental ground for the value of freedom but failing to offer any attempt at such a proof in what he takes to be the most likely place for it, *Groundwork* III. At this point the value of freedom is left hanging as a mere assertion on Kant's part. But, as Guyer now argues, Kant may be able to argue for the value of freedom based upon the fact of freedom as a capacity in us.

2 On Freedom as a Capacity in Us

The previous section started by presenting Guyer's praise of what he sees as Kant's early attempts to provide an empirical rather that a transcendental basis for the claim that freedom is of value. Guyer was skeptical that Kant could successfully directly prove, or even that he tried to directly prove, the value of freedom through any transcendental argument. I now turn to Guyer's claim that Kant tries to prove the transcendental reality of our capacity for freedom, which he now takes to be a step toward proving the value of freedom.

As with value, Guyer is also skeptical about the use of transcendental idealism in any proof of our capacity for freedom. His statement rejecting transcendental idealism in this regard could hardly be more direct:

> Kant's defense of freedom in this sense [of alternative possibilities as a metaphysical possibility] [...] depends on his transcendental idealism, a doctrine the defense and even the meaning of which remains controversial more than two centuries after its publication. This doctrine is the basis for Kant's confidence that 'ought implies can', that is, that we are always free to

---

Understanding and Philosophy: The Strategy of Kant's *Groundwork*", in *Philosophie in synthetischer Absicht*, ed. by Marcelo Stamm, Stuttgart 1988, 271–298).

choose to do the right thing no matter what our upbringing, prior choices, and so on might appear to imply. But my view is that we can let it remain an empirical question just how far human beings are free to preserve and promote freedom of choice and action in their intra- and interpersonal doings while still appreciating Kant's account of the foundation of all duties in the intrinsic and unconditional value of getting to set our own ends free from unwarranted constraint from others and even from unwarranted constraint by our own inclinations.[17]

This is a skepticism about the appropriateness of transcendental idealism regarding the attribution of freedom to ourselves, the mere claim that we are able to choose and are responsible for our own actions. Guyer ultimately rejects what he takes to be Kant's transcendental proof of freedom, offering instead at least one way in which an empirically-based attribution of freedom would be sufficient for morality. His article "Proving Ourselves Free" holds that our common practices of attributing moral responsibility to others and our first-person experience of moral deliberation is enough to ground and justify our attribution of freedom to ourselves. No proof of indeterminism is needed, and in fact, for purposes of attributing moral responsibility to others, the causal link between an action and a person's character that holds under determinism is a reinforcement rather than an obstacle.[18] The practices of imputation take into account empirical factors such as sobriety and drunkenness, and presumably knowledge and ability and likely motives, as part of the everyday judgment holding others responsible. Guyer does take Kant in *Groundwork* III to try to prove from the first person, each for ourselves, that we are each free, but this proof, if successful, would hold only for each individual's self-attribution of freedom. (The details of the proof will be discussed below.) Since we have no access to any other minds we could not apply any analogous proof to those others. But Guyer has presented a way in which our attributions of freedom for moral purposes can be understood empirically. This possibility of an empirically understood conception of freedom, one that does not require any indeterminacy or independence from causal laws, will be cited again later in this paper.

Given that Guyer takes Kant's empirical claim about freedom in relation to moral responsibility to apply to others, he sees one task of *Groundwork* III to prove from the first person point of view that each of us are free. Guyer also held *Groundwork* III to be the location of any transcendental proof of the value of freedom, although he thought that the actual argument Kant presented sidestepped that issue. The transcendent claim that Guyer now attributes to Kant in ethics is only that we human beings have free wills that are independent of causal determination, not that there is any transcendently real value. Here I will present this claim as Guyer

---

17 Guyer, *Virtues*, v.
18 Guyer, "Proving Ourselves Free", in Guyer, *Virtues*, 146–162.

describes it in the recent book *Kant on the Rationality of Morality*, where he also makes the claim rejecting his earlier interpretation of the transcendental status of the value of freedom.[19] Guyer takes Kant to be a semantic realist, one who claims that moral principles are capable of truth and falsity and are in fact true. The most general moral principles such as the categorical imperative and general principles of right and virtue are true for all, while more specific claims about moral duty would be constructed from those general principles using some specific empirical information. But what would ground the truth of these moral principles? Guyer admits here to an ontological realism about human freedom. He also takes back his earlier view that he now admits was a value realism about the value of freedom.[20] His updated view is to reject the realism of value for a realism of freedom itself, "the fact that every human being has a will of his or her own", and allow that moral value is not transcendentally real.[21] Guyer holds the fact of free will

> is not a mysterious moral fact, or a value that somehow exists in the universe independently of our act of valuing it. It is simply a fact that cannot be denied on pain of self-contradiction, since, Kant assumes, in some way we always recognize it even when by our actions we would deny it. Whether Kant has succeeded in demonstrating this fact is a question; but there is no question that he regards our possession of wills as a fact from which moral theory must begin.[22]

Guyer takes this fact of a will to be the ground of morality through the use of the principle of non-contradiction, a claim to which I will return. Directly important here is his claim that Kant assumes that free will is a transcendent fact (or, as Guyer had put it, a transcendentally realist claim).

This is the point to make clear precisely what conception of freedom Guyer has in mind in these discussions. The freedom at issue for Guyer is a freedom to choose for or against the law, to set our own ends without being determined to any particular ends, and to choose good or evil, the right thing or the wrong thing. This libertarian view of freedom emphasizes that the will is not subject to any causal determinants of its actions. Guyer rejects the kind of freedom that Kant sometimes described that is limited to choices determined by reason, that is, morally correct choices stemming from the application of the categorical imperative. Guyer repeatedly invokes the Ulrich/Sidgwick objection to that kind of freedom which limits

---

19 Guyer, *Rationality*, 64.
20 Guyer references as an earlier work that took Kant to be a value realist "The Value of Reason and the Value of Freedom", *Ethics* 109, 1998, 22–35, a long review of Korsgaard's *Creating the Kingdom of Ends*.
21 Guyer, *Rationality*, 64.
22 Ibid.

freedom to rationally determined decisions[23] and prefers the kind of freedom that Kant alludes to in the *Religion within the Boundaries of Mere Reason* as a choice for or against the moral law. When freedom is of value, for Guyer it is the expansive libertarian freedom described here. Guyer holds that Kant needs to prove this libertarian conception of free will in *Groundwork* III.

I now turn to Kant's argument in *Groundwork* III. There is not enough space here to detail the many interpretations and many steps involved in this complex argument. Guyer has discussed it in numerous places as well. Here I will focus on the crucial step of the argument when Kant tries to escape from what he describes as a circle by invoking the claim that every human being should readily be able to distinguish the way that objects affect us from the way that they may be in themselves (GMS, AA 04: 450–453). While there is little doubt that Kant intends in some way to invoke transcendental idealism, the precise claims that Kant makes must be noted in order to see what Kant intends to draw from that doctrine.

Guyer takes Kant to be broadly claiming that we human beings must view ourselves as things-in-ourselves completely independent of how we may appear. I take Kant's claim to have a much more limited target, namely, the *faculty of reason* itself rather than any being in ourselves completely distinct from how we appear in nature. The key passage in the argument Kant provides in *Groundwork* III about the basis for a two-standpoint claim on our self-description is when Kant says "a human being really finds in himself a capacity by which he distinguishes himself from all other things, even from himself insofar as he is affected by objects, and that is reason. This, as pure self activity [...]" (GMS, AA 04: 452). The passage continues by invoking the understanding as well, with both faculties acting as sources for concepts or ideas that differ from mere representation arising from sense. Guyer glosses the latter part of this quotation this way (italicizing Guyer's words) "[...] as he is affected by objects' *(that is, himself as appearance)*, 'and that is reason', *which is understood in turn as* 'pure self activity' — *or will*".[24] It is worth noting that Kant does not use the term "will" anywhere in that paragraph. His emphasis is on reason as an active source of ideas and, more importantly, a source of causal laws. Since human beings see their own faculty of reason as an active source of ideas and principles that cannot be understood to stem passively from sensation, they are able to view themselves from two standpoints. Human beings can see themselves as subject to laws of nature as belonging to the world of sense and "as belonging to the intelligible world, under laws which, being independent of nature, are not empirical but grounded merely in reason" (GMS, AA 04: 452). What Kant is citing here as pure self activity is not a will

---

23 For example, in Guyer, "Proving", 154–155.
24 Quoted from Kant, with Guyer emendations in italics, *Rationality*, 65.

that can determine ends for itself or decide for or against the moral law but the faculty of reason itself that provides that moral law. Reason as provider of ideas and principles and not will as an ability to choose is the part of our self-ascription that cannot be attributed to appearances. I take Kant to be invoking a claim that we are allowed to question whether there are any sources of our representations that cannot be attributed to appearances, and that his candidate is the faculty of reason. He does not here widen this ascription to libertarian freedom of the will or even to ourselves as things-in-themselves more broadly (except in the general sense that *if* we had some ground for explaining something about our appearances that we could not attribute to appearance, *then* we would be authorized to assume it).

Now Guyer does recognize that Kant mentions reason. But he thinks first that Kant moves from this attribution of reason to the more general claim about us as beings in ourselves. For example, in the recent *Idealism in Modern Philosophy*, he says: "We also have insight into the self-activity or spontaneity of our own pure reason" which leads us to the concept of an intelligible world, which "is an assertion of real idealism, that is, of the intelligent and therefore mental nature of our being at its most fundamental level".[25] Guyer thinks that Kant is not entitled to take this step, however, for various reasons that I need not repeat here. The issue at stake is not whether Kant is entitled to make this move in his argument but whether he does make this move in his argument. I grant that much of his immediate language appears to invoke our "membership" in an "world of the understanding". But as Kant proceeds in *Groundwork* III he clarifies that this is merely a standpoint we can take that allows us to see ourselves as subject to the causality of nature as well as the causality of reason. He minimizes the claim about the activity of reason to it being the source of the moral law. While Kant certainly uses language about separate worlds (the world of the understanding and the world of sense), he also limits the import of that language by talking about two standpoints or two orders of things — which I take to be of the *same* things, namely humans in nature (e.g. GMS, AA 04: 457). His causality regarding moral actions are "in accordance with principles of an intelligible world, of which he knows nothing more than that in it reason alone, and indeed pure reason independent of sensibility, gives the law" (GMS, AA 04: 457). Further, even to talk about a "world" of understanding is "only a standpoint that reason sees itself constrained to take outside appearances in order to think of itself as practical" which of course seems to involve a conception of "the whole of rational beings as things in themselves" but only in its "formal condition, that is, of the universality of maxims of the will as law and so of the autonomy of the will, which alone is compatible with its freedom" (GMS, AA 04: 458). In the final

---

25 Guyer, Paul, and Horstmann, Rolf-Peter, *Idealism in Modern Philosophy*, Oxford 2023, 64.

paragraph of *Groundwork* III, Kant even alludes to the way that reason creates ideas for itself in order to posit an unconditioned when faced with a series of conditions, leading both theoretical and practical reason to "assume" the "unconditionally necessary" in order to satisfy reason itself, although it can never make an unconditioned law comprehensible to itself. Guyer himself notes that as Kant proceeds in his discussion in *Groundwork* III after providing the claim about the two standpoints, Kant "seems to weaken the initial argument of Section III" and to "step back from the brink".[26] If one reads the argument of *Groundwork* III as a whole, however, properly emphasizing the limitations Kant invokes and the way that he applies the two standpoints only to the obligation we human beings have to the moral law stemming from reason, then Kant is not weakening his argument at all. The argument is properly only centered on reason as the source of another kind of causal law — the moral law — that we human beings take ourselves to be subject to in our empirical choices.[27] All that we are entitled to assume from the two standpoints argument is that reason is an active source of the moral law that is obligatory for us.

Guyer of course notices that Kant invokes reason. But Guyer takes Kant to not be entitled to any claim that we must understand reason independently of appearances. He claims that Kant equivocates between reason as empirically observable, for example when we build our structures according to reason rather than instinct, and reason that cannot be empirically observed.[28] The former is attributable to us because of our activities in nature and distinguishes us from animals; the latter resides in our "real selves". Here I think Guyer is mistaken in his interpretation. Rather than an equivocation, this is instead an important claim that helps to illuminate Kant's argument. We do observe ourselves behaving rationally, both in moral and in non-moral situations. When we attribute this rationality to ourselves, we are attributing to reason itself some independence from nature, in that the principles of reason, the way that reason underlies logical relations, the demand of reason for consistency, etc, are themselves attributed to a timeless structure of reason. We

---

26 Guyer, Paul, Kant's Groundwork for the Metaphysics of Morals: A Reader's Guide, New York 2007, 167.
27 These interpretive issues are of course much more complicated than space allows for in this paper. I make this argument in more detail in two papers: Rauscher, Frederick, "Freedom and Reason in Groundwork III" (in J. Timmermann, ed., *Kant's Groundwork of the Metaphysics of Morals: A Critical Guide*, Cambridge 2009, 203–223) and Rauscher, Frederick, "Die äußerste Grenze aller praktischen Philosophie und die Einschränkungen der Deduktion in *Grundlegung* III" (in *Kants Begründung von Freiheit und Moral in Grundlegung III*, ed. by D. Schönecker, Münster 2015, 215–229), both of which are largely incorporated into my book *Naturalism and Realism in Kant's Ethics* (Cambridge, 2015).
28 Guyer, *Guide*, 159–160.

cannot empirically observe that structure of reason any more than we can empirically observe mathematical truths. We must see the effects of reason on our actions as a kind of pure activity that plays a role in determining our empirical actions yet that cannot be explained merely according to natural law. The very fact that we take our empirical actions to be effects of reason means that we see our actions as caused by reason in a way distinguishable from laws of nature that demands another ground of explanation. That explanation is to attribute an independence to reason so that its principles are not themselves subject to determination by laws of nature (laws of appearances).

How does this emphasis on reason relate to free will? Here, contra Guyer, I bite the bullet and accept that Kant takes a free will (or free power of choice) to be one that is determined by the moral law. If we are allowed to attribute a different kind of causality to reason — a causality in which a principle or law plays a role in determining our empirical decisions — then we can allow for an empirical power of choice in nature to be deemed free to the extent that it is determined by reason. Kant claims that freedom is "only an idea of reason" (GMS, AA 04: 455). This independence of reason is the basis for attributions of freedom of will. "The rightful claim to freedom of will made even by common human reason is based on the consciousness and the granted presupposition of the independence of reason from merely subjectively determining causes" (GMS, AA 04: 457). Reason's independence is the ground of any attribution of freedom to the will. Recall that Kant rejects any claim that freedom could be understood as independence from laws but must be understood as not lawless but causality in accordance with another kind of law other than laws of nature (GMS, AA 04: 446). I take Kant seriously to claim that a libertarian freedom of the will, one in which there is a choice not determined by either the moral law or a law of nature, is lawless in this sense. The proper conception of will we can draw from *Groundwork* III is a will under moral laws that stem from reason. Thus the basis of any claim to freedom of the will depends upon a prior claim to the freedom of reason itself as source of the moral laws that fill in as causes beyond the limits of causality of natural law.

This interpretation of *Groundwork* III should not be seen in isolation. We can look back to the First *Critique* and ahead to the Second *Critique* to see that Kant invokes reason in similar contexts. Looking backward, but without time for detailed assessment, note that Kant's resolution to the Third Antinomy also invokes reason, not will, as the faculty that possesses free causality, and cites its production of imperatives as evidence (KrV, A 547/B 575, with references to reason as cause throughout the remainder of the resolution). Looking ahead, Guyer also invokes the Fact of Reason to support his claim that freedom of the will comes first as a basis for morality.[29] But Kant is clear that freedom is a result of the Fact of Reason, not the Fact of Reason itself: our practical cognition "cannot start from freedom" but instead "it is the moral law ... that first offers itself to us" (KpV, AA 05: 29). In the passage that Guyer invokes Kant bases the claim to freedom on reason's providing the moral law to us: "We can become aware of pure practical laws just as we are aware of pure theoretical principles, by attending to the necessity with which reason prescribes them to us", and further, "one would never have ventured to introduce freedom into science had not the moral law, and with it practical reason, come in and forced this concept upon us" (KpV, AA 05: 30). "Consciousness of this fundamental law may be called a fact of reason" (KpV, AA 05: 31) Kant continues. We are not directly aware of our free will but are aware that our will is free only because we are aware of the demand of reason to comport our will to the law of reason, experienced by us as a categorical imperative.

Allow me to draw from all these passages the main point regarding reason and will. Contra Guyer's claims, in *Groundwork* III Kant is not primarily or solely — and perhaps not even at all — claiming that we have a will considered as an ability to set ends or to choose between good and evil or to be free from causal law. For the will to be free is for the will to be subject to the causal laws of reason. Reason itself must be considered as free or self-active in order to produce ideas and principles that are not derived from but are applied to the world of sense. Kant stresses the activity of reason as the ground for claims to independence from natural causality. If anything is free as a fact about human beings, it is reason rather than will.

I started this section by discussing Guyer's distaste for the transcendent as an ontology that requires non-spatial and non-temporal things in themselves. Because he views free will seen as free in a libertarian sense, able to choose good or evil, to set ends without limitation, in short, to be independent of causal determinism, he sees this will as a property of a person in herself outside of nature. It is certainly problematic to conceive of a person's power of choice as a facet of a non-spatial, non-temporal essence of a person in herself that is yet able to decide in context particular actions in space and time. But if instead the way to understand free will is only when it is determined in accordance with a causality of reason, through a standpoint that invokes reason as a cause, then the free will can be located in nature in space and time, and only the causal source in reason needs to be explained in a way that would go beyond mere natural causality. It is not anywhere near as problematic to conceive of the faculty of reason as independent of space and time, given that the timeless nature of the principles of reason already point in that direction. The empirical will can be seen as

---

29 Guyer, *Rationality*, 65.

subject to two kinds of causality simultaneously — the causality of nature through laws of nature and the causality of freedom through moral laws.

3 The Source of Value

Given the assessments of free will and reason just provided, and in line with Guyer's earlier claim, it is clear that Kant does not intend to provide a deduction of the value of freedom, or any moral value, in *Groundwork* III. Yet although Guyer would have preferred otherwise, Kant also cannot offer an empirical defense of the value of freedom. In this final brief section I will suggest that Guyer's more recent work on the rationality of morality provides a transcendental ground for moral value.

In the book *Kant on the Rationality of Morality*, Guyer renounces his earlier view that Kant offers a metaphysical realism about moral value.[30] He is now committed to a claim that reason in application to humans as acting agents generates the moral law and, presumably, moral value. He is clear that he understands Kant's use of reason in morality to be a specific application of a more general reason that straddles both theoretical and practical applications.[31] This reason requires universality and noncontradiction. When Guyer prepares to show how Kant grounds the moral law in reason, he claims that one must go beyond the principle of noncontradiction itself to include some content because as a purely formal principle, the principle of non-contradiction must be applied to some content to yield any potential contradiction. This is certainly true. Reason can demand consistency, but *what* must be consistent depends upon particular content. Guyer takes the content to be a fact that human beings are capable of setting their own ends, which then grounds the fundamental principle of morality, which he paraphrases as "we not contradict the nature of human beings as rational agents, capable of setting their own ends".[32] This makes Kant's reasoning dependent upon the prior claim that we human beings are free, which Guyer sees as a transcendentally realist claim about human beings as they are in themselves.[33]

I follow Guyer partway here. First, I take it that reason's use of the principle of non-contradiction has content for practical purposes when potential actions, or to be more precise maxims for potential actions, are assessed in accordance with it.

---

30 Guyer, *Rationality*, 63–64.
31 Guyer, *Rationality*, 3.
32 Guyer, *Rationality*, 11–14.
33 Guyer, *Rationality*, 65.

The merely formal, contentless principle of non-contradiction is expressed by Kant for practical application as the universal law formula of the categorical imperative, which tests maxims for potential contradictions. Second, I would describe the work of reason not as applied to human beings' capacity to set ends but to the concept of any rational being as one who sets ends, with the question of whether it applies to human beings left for a further step (Guyer approaches the issue this way at times).[34] Third, while Guyer sees the human capacity to set ends as a fact, I would see it as a self-conception we take on from the first-person perspective. We are active beings who adopt the standpoint of deliberation on our actions and our ends whether or not such self-ascription is ultimately deceptive. These minor differences, however, are not important here.

Although Guyer does not state this explicitly, I think he holds now that moral value results from the application of reason to the fact that human beings have wills and are capable of setting ends. Since moral value is not attached to that fact, it must be a result of the synthetic operation of reason in applying its principle of non-contradiction to that fact. Moral value is thus not metaphysically real but metaphysically ideal or anti-real, stemming from the operation of reason. And since this value is not contingent upon anything except the application of reason, the ground of this value can be understood to be transcendentally grounded. No deliberative agent with a self-conception as rationally deliberative can have the kind of moral experience it has without being obligated to reason's categorical imperative and with it the value reason imposes. Reason's practical application carries with it normativity since, as rational beings, we experience our rationality as a demand for rational consistency. This kind of transcendental ground does not require any non-natural ontology beyond a conception of reason itself having a special status as the ground of law independent of natural law.

4 Conclusion

Guyer has resisted the transcendental in Kant for most of his career, favoring whenever possible interpretations that are grounded empirically or that do not require claims about things in themselves radically different from the way we experience objects — and ourselves — in nature. I have suggested in this paper that his worries about the need for transcendental freedom of the will can be allayed under an interpretation that emphasizes instead the transcendental independence of reason as

---

34 See Guyer, *Rationality*, 17.

a faculty that grounds the moral law that can determine the empirical will (or power of choice). This interpretation would allow for a larger role for an empirically informed conception of freedom and moral responsibility along the lines that Guyer advocates. This freedom is also of importance from the practical, first-person point of view that we take up as moral agents, where we identify as rational beings because we experience the fact of reason as a categorical imperative and subsequently see ourselves as not only obligated to follow that moral law but also as constrained to value other rational beings through that imposition by reason. Value is thus not transcendentally real but transcendentally grounded, and requires no claim about human beings as non-natural things in themselves radically different from our experience. This paper has assessed Guyer's claims about the empirical and transcendental in Kant's ethics and pointed the way to a resolution of some of the problems Guyer found.

References

Allison, Henry (2007). "Comments on Guyer." *Inquiry* 50, 480–488.
Guyer, Paul (1987). *Kant and the Claims of Knowledge*, Cambridge.
Guyer, Paul (1988). "Self-Understanding and Philosophy: The Strategy of Kant's *Groundwork*." In *Philosophie in synthetischer Absicht*, ed. by Marcelo Stamm, Stuttgart, 271–298.
Guyer, Paul (1998). "The Value of Reason and the Value of Freedom." *Ethics* 109, 22–35.
Guyer, Paul (2006). *Kant*, New York.
Guyer, Paul (2007). *Kant's Groundwork for the Metaphysics of Morals: A Reader's Guide*, New York.
Guyer, Paul (2007). "Naturalistic and Transcendental Moments in Kant's Moral Philosophy." *Inquiry* 50, 444–464.
Guyer, Paul (2016a). *The Virtues of Freedom*, Oxford.
Guyer, Paul (2016b). "Proving Ourselves Free." In *Virtues of Freedom*, 146–162.
Guyer, Paul (2017). "Transcendental Idealism: What and Why?" In *The Palgrave Kant Handbook*, ed. by M. Altman, London, 71–90.
Guyer, Paul (2019). *Kant on the Rationality of Morality*, Cambridge.
Guyer, Paul, and Rolf-Peter Horstmann (2023). *Idealism in Modern Philosophy*, Oxford.
Korsgaard, Christine (1997). *Creating the Kingdom of Ends*, Cambridge.
Rauscher, Frederick (2009). "Freedom and Reason in *Groundwork* III." In *Kant's Groundwork of the Metaphysics of Morals: A Critical Guide*, ed. by J. Timmermann, Cambridge, 203–223.
Rauscher, Frederick (2015). "Die äußerste Grenze aller praktischen Philosophie und die Einschränkungen der Deduktion in *Grundlegung* III." In *Kants Begründung von Freiheit und Moral in Grundlegung III*, ed. by D. Schönecker, Münster, 215–229.
Rauscher, Frederick (2015). *Naturalism and Realism in Kant's Ethics*, Cambridge.

Lucas Thorpe
Guyer, Sellars and Kant on the Dignity and Value of Freedom

Abstract: Paul Guyer is well known for defending the claim that freedom, understood as the capacity to set ends, is Kant's fundamental value. In contrast, I have developed a reading of Kant's ethics that places autonomy and community at the heart of Kant's ethics. At the heart of my account is a conception of autonomy understood as what I call the capacity for sovereignty. I argue that these two positions can be made compatible. To do this involves making a distinction between the concepts of dignity and value and arguing that although autonomy, understood as the capacity for sovereignty, is the source of the dignity of humanity, this is compatible with the claim that the ultimate value for Kant is freedom understood as the capacity to set ends. To explain how this is possible I appeal to Wilfred Sellars Kantian account of the moral point of view in *Science and Metaphysics*.

Keywords: Sellars, Guyer, humanity, freedom

Paul Guyer is well known for defending the claim that freedom, understood as the capacity to set ends, is Kant's fundamental value. In contrast, I have developed a reading of Kant's ethics that places autonomy and community at the heart of Kant's ethics.[1] At the heart of my account is a conception of autonomy understood as what I call in this paper the capacity for sovereignty. Until now I have always implicitly assumed that Guyer and I were offering alternative, competing accounts of Kant's understanding of freedom and ultimate value. In this paper, however, I will argue that these two positions can be made compatible. To do this involves making a distinction between the concepts of dignity and value and arguing that although autonomy, understood as the capacity for sovereignty, is the source of the dignity of humanity, this is compatible with the claim that the ultimate value for Kant is freedom understood as the capacity to set ends. To explain how this is possible I appeal to Wilfred Sellars Kantian account of the moral point of view in Science and Metaphysics.[2] Sellars argues that morality must be universal both in

---

1 See Thorpe 2010, 2011, 2013 & 2018.
2 Guyer's first full-time teaching position was at Pittsburgh (1973–1978) where he overlapped with Sellars — although according to Guyer they did not really interact philosophically. My first serious encounter with Sellars was when we read *Science and Metaphysics* in a graduate seminar

its form and content; it must come from all and apply to all. For Sellars, volitions are universal in their form if they are the expression of we-intentions. In terms of universality in content, however, Sellars argues that the most fundamental we-intention, the one that has what he calls underived categorical validity, is some form of the utilitarian principle of the form "We intend that our welfare be maximized." With regard to the content, I believe (following Guyer) that the promotion of freedom, understood as the capacity to set and pursue ends, is a far more plausible candidate for the universal content of such an underived categorial we-intention than welfare. However, we are still left with the questions of why we should adopt the moral point of view. And here I will argue that what compels us, morally, to adopt the moral point of view is the recognition of the dignity of humanity, understood in terms of the capacity for sovereignty. It is autonomy understood as the capacity of sovereignty that is the source of our dignity, and this is what compels us to adopt the moral point of view. This is compatible, however, with Guyer's claim that what we ultimately value, from within the moral point of view is freedom, understood as a capacity to set (and pursue) ends.

This paper has five sections. In the first I briefly outline Guyer's account of the value of freedom as the capacity to set ends. In the second I explain my understanding of autonomy as the capacity for sovereignty. In the third I explain Sellars account of the moral point of view and argue that freedom understood as the capacity to set ends is a better candidate for the content of the underived categorical we-intention than (universal) welfare. I conclude the section by suggesting that a more plausible candidate for Kant's account of what has absolute value from within the moral point of view is the idea of being a member of a realm of ends. In the fourth I argue that what compels us to adopt the moral point of view is the dignity of humanity. In the final section I briefly discuss and defend the distinction between dignity and value.

1 Guyer on the Value of Freedom

Today it is common for philosophers to suggest that there is an exclusive disjunction between teleological and deontological ethical theories and to present Kantian ethics as a paradigm example of a deontological ethical theory. This way of classifying ethical theories as either deontological or teleological is relatively

---

at Penn that Guyer gave in the 1990s on 20th century anglophone appropriations of Kant's theoretical philosophy.

recent. The word "deontology" seems to have been coined in the early nineteenth century by Jeremy Bentham, but through much of the nineteenth century and into the early twentieth century the word deontology was just used as a highfalutin way of saying "ethical theory". In the late nineteenth century, however, many anglophone philosophers attempted to introduce ways of categorizing moral theories into broad opposing camps. And by the 1930s, many philosophers in the English-speaking world came to think that the broadest distinction was between those theories that started off with some conception of the good as the most basic moral concept, and those that rejected such a starting point and insisted that we had to start with an account of what is right that is independent of any account of what is good. And it soon became the norm to refer to those theories that started with a theory of the good as basic as 'teleological theories' and those that rejected such a starting point 'deontological theories'. Louden (1996) and Philips (2019, 10) both suggest that these terms were first used in print in the contemporary sense by C.D. Broad in 1930.[3]

Guyer (as we shall see, like Sellars) is one of the most influential proponents of a (more) teleological reading of Kant's ethics arguing that the value of freedom plays a central, foundational role in his moral theory.[4] Now Guyer recognizes that Kant sometimes seems to give arguments that imply a purely deontological position. Thus, for example, Guyer (2000b, 132f) argues that in the *Critique of Practical Reason* (KpV, AA 05: 64) Kant suggests that because the fundamental principle of morality must be universal and necessary, if we assume (as Kant seems to do in this passage) that any determination of the good independently of the moral law could only be based on the feeling of pleasure and hence would be empirical, then

---

[3] "I would first divide ethical theories into two classes, which I will call respectively *deontological* and *teleological*. Deontological theories hold that there are ethical propositions of the form: 'Such and such a kind of action would always be right (or wrong) in such and such circumstances, no matter what its consequences might be.'...Teleological theories hold that the rightness or wrongness of an action is always determined by its tendency to promote certain consequences which are intrinsically good or bad." (Broad, 1930, 206f)

[4] I equivocate here, as it is not clear whether Guyer ultimately wants to defend a (purely) teleological interpretation of Kant or whether he wants to reject the dichotomy and suggest that there are both teleological and deontological aspects to Kant's position. Thus Guyer (2000b, 133f) argues that "In the end, however, it is probably better to say Kant's theory undercuts the traditional distinction [between teleological and deontological theories]: his final view is surely that the freedom that is intrinsically valuable is freedom that governs itself by law, or autonomy, and this conception incorporates ideas of both value and duty in itself. No end that is not licensed by the unconditional constraint of the moral law can be good, but the unconditional constraint furnished by the moral law is in turn the condition necessary to preserve and enhance the unconditional value of freedom itself."

the fundamental principle of morality must be one that cannot presuppose any conception of the good or of value.[5] Guyer argues, however, that Kant ultimately rejects the assumption that the only candidate for something that can determine the good independently of the moral law is pleasure, for he is committed to the intrinsic value of freedom. One piece of evidence that Guyer frequently cites, to support this claim, are a pair of passages from the Lectures on Ethics where Kant argues that, "if all creatures had a faculty of choice bound to sensuous desires, the world would have no value; the inner value of the world, the *summum bonum*, is the freedom to act in accordance with a faculty of choice that is not necessitated. Freedom is therefore the inner value of the world." (V-Mo/Mrong 27: 1482)[6] This passage clearly distinguishes between the purported value of pleasure and the value of freedom, and offers a potential strategy for offering a teleological reading of Kant's ethics according to which the moral law demands that we promote freedom. However, as this claim is only found in his lectures, it is not clear how much weight to put on it. And, as Rauscher (2018, 167) points out, it is quite possible that this passage is a rhetorical flourish aimed at his young students to get them to appreciate the importance of freedom, rather than a considered espousal of his basic theory. So, it is not clear how much interpretive weight this passage can support.

Guyer offers a number of arguments for the claim that the value of freedom (understood as the capacity to set ends) is prior to the moral law. I will focus on one of them.

Guyer's argument begins by noting that Kant "recognizes that rational human action must always have an end intended to be realized in nature" (2005b, 170) and he argues that this implies that Kant must be committed to the existence of a universally valid end. Thus Guyer explains that Kant's moral philosophy is

> teleological from the outset insofar as it is founded upon the argument that the adoption of any principle without an end to which adherence to this principle would be the means would be irrational; that a universally valid principle or practical law requires a universally valid end, or an end with absolute worth; that particular ends contingently suggested by inclination obviously do not have absolute worth; and that the only alternative to them is humanity itself, which must have absolute worth and must be the end advanced by adherence to the moral law. (Guyer, 2005b, 173f)

---

[5] For an alternative reading of the passage see Thorpe (2019). Here I argue that in the passage from the *Critique of Practical Reason* under discussion Kant makes it clear that the priority of the right over the good is merely methodological.

[6] The same claim is also found in the Collins version of the lectures. Rauscher (2018, 155) finds 8 citations of these passage in Guyer's published writings.

And Guyer believes that what Kant means by "humanity" in this context is freedom understood as the capacity to set ends. So, he concludes that the universally valid end of morality is the capacity to set ends. Now, I am convinced by Guyer's argument here that Kantian ethics requires a universally valid end and that this universally valid end cannot be happiness. Thus, like Guyer and Sellars, I am attracted to a broadly teleological interpretation of Kantian ethics. However, I am not convinced that this universally valid end must be humanity, understood in terms of the capacity to set ends. For the idea of being a member of a realm of ends seems an equally plausible candidate for such a universally valid end.[7]

To convince his readers that Kant identifies humanity with the capacity to set ends Guyer frequently appeals to a pair of passages in the *Metaphysics of Morals*. Thus he argues,

> Kant says that humanity is the feature of human beings by which they alone are capable of setting themselves ends (MS, TL, Introduction, section V, AA 06: 387), or that "The capacity to set oneself an end — any end whatsoever — is what characterizes humanity (as opposed to animality)" (section VIII, AA 06: 392). If we plug this definition into the formula of humanity from the Groundwork, we get the prescription always treat the capacity to set ends, any ends whatsoever, whether in your own person or that of any other, as an end, never merely as a means. (Guyer 2016c, 88)[8]

Now this is a perfectly plausible way of reading these texts. But it is not mandated and in general we should be cautious about plugging in a (seeming) definition from one text into a principle in another text published more than ten years previously. In addition, there are clearly passages that tell against such a reading. Thus in the *Critique of Practical Reason*, in a passage clearly linked to the discussion of the formula of humanity of the *Groundwork*, Kant argues, that,

> The moral law is holy (inviolable). A human being is indeed unholy enough but the humanity in his person must be holy to him. In the whole of creation everything one wants and over which one has any power can also be used merely as a means; a human being alone, and with him every rational creature, is an end in itself: by virtue of the autonomy of his freedom he is the subject of the moral law, which is holy. Just because of this every will, even every person's own will directed to himself, is restricted to the condition of agreement with

---

7 For an alternative view see Vatansever (2021) who distinguishes the end set by the moral law for individual humans from the end set for the human species.
8 In just two of volumes of collected papers, Guyer cites at least one of these passages in twelve separate papers. And there are many other citations in other volumes. So these passages are quite possibly Guyer's favorite passages in Kant's corpus. See: Guyer (2005b, 175), (2005c, 154), (2005d, 201), (2005e, 244), (2005f, 367), (2016a, 82), (2016b, 58), (2016c, 88), (2016d, 12), (2016e, 106), (2016f, 137), (2016g, 211).

the autonomy of the rational being, that is to say, such a being is not to be subjected to any purpose that is not possible in accordance **with a law that could arise from the will of the affected subject himself**; hence this subject is to be used never merely as a means but as at the same time an end. We righty attribute this condition even to the divine will with respect to the rational beings in the world as its creatures, inasmuch as it rests on their personality, by which alone they are ends in themselves. (KpV, AA 05: 87 – bolding added)

Here Kant identifies humanity with what I call the capacity of sovereignty (the capacity to give laws). And I think that this passage has far more evidential weight for what Kant means by "humanity" than the passages Guyer quotes from the *Metaphysics of Morals*, as this passage is about why human beings are ends in themselves, while the passages from the *Metaphysics of Morals* have to do with cultivating our natural talents. And I think that there is a way of making these passages compatible. For Kant is systematically ambiguous in the way he uses the word humanity. For in some places he makes a threefold distinction between personality (autonomy, understood as what I call a capacity for sovereignty), humanity (understood as our capacity to set ends) and our animality. But in other places he uses humanity to refer to someone who has personality, humanity and animality. This is not an aberration as Kant has an annoying tendency to use the same word for the genus and one of the species falling under it.[9] So humanity in the narrow sense (as the capacity to set ends) is an aspect of humanity in the broad sense because personality presupposes the capacity to set ends.

I suggest that Guyer conflates the idea of an end-in-itself with the idea of necessarily valid end. On my reading these two notions need to be distinguished. The appeal to humanity as an end-in-itself in is not supposed to offer an account of the value of humanity as something that that is supposed to be the necessary object of moral will, but to the dignity of personality (understood as the capacity for sovereignty) that necessitates us to take the moral point of view. If this interpretation of the formula of humanity is correct, then this would leave the task of identifying the universally valid end of morality to the third formulation of the categorical imperative, where Kant introduces the idea of the realm of ends.

---

9 So, for example, Kant sometimes uses "Reason" or "the Understanding" as the name of the genus, of which "Reason", "Understanding" and "Judgment" are species. He sometimes uses "Concept" to refer to the genus of which "Concepts" and "Ideas" are species, etc.

2 Autonomy as Sovereignty

In this section, I will argue that for Kant autonomy involves the capacity to give laws that bind both oneself and others. And I name this the capacity for sovereignty.[10] In Sellarsian terms we may say that such a capacity should be thought of as a capacity to form intentions that bind both ourselves and others, or, in other words, the capacity to form we-intentions. To be autonomous, in this sense is a necessary membership condition for being a citizen in a realm of ends. Thus, Kant explains that "[a] rational being belongs as a member to the realm of ends when he gives universal laws in it but is also himself subject to these laws" (GMS, AA 04: 433). And Kant also thinks autonomy, understood as the capacity to give laws for a realm of ends, is what makes such a community itself possible. Thus, he argues that,

> [I]n this way a world of rational beings (*mundus intelligibilis*) as a realm of ends is possible, through the giving of their own laws by all persons as members (GMS, AA 04: 438)

Note that here Kant identifies the notion of realm of ends with the idea of an intelligible world. And so, it is helpful to read this claim in light of Kant's claims about the idea of an intelligible world in his metaphysics lectures. Kant believes that the idea of an intelligible world is the idea of a community of individuals in interaction and thinks that it is possible to conceive of a community of individuals in interaction only if we think of the members of the community as governed by laws, and we can think of the members of a community as governed by laws only if we think of each individual member of the community as the source or giver of these laws. Kant believes that a world is essentially unified, for it is this unity that distinguishes the idea of a world from that of a mere multitude. In addition, he believes that a multitude of individual substances can only be unified or 'held together' by laws. So, the idea of a world is the idea of a multitude of individuals unified by laws. Now, if the unity of a world is to be 'intrinsic' to the world, rather than merely existing in the mind of some ideal observer observing the world — that is, if there is to be real interaction between the members of the world rather than a mere constant conjunction or harmony between the state of one substance and that of another (à la Hume or Leibniz) — then the members of the world must be responsible for the unity of the world, and Kant believes that this is possible only if each individual member of the world is the source of, or 'the giver of,' the laws that provide the world with its unity. That is, in the language of his mature

---

10 I'm not sure if this is the best way to name this capacity. Other possible names might be "the capacity for citizenship" or "the capacity for personality".

ethics, we can think of a community of individuals in interaction only if we think of each individual member of the community as autonomous. And to be autonomous is not merely, or even primarily, to rule oneself, but rather to be the source of the laws of a possible community, to be a co-legislator in an ideal republic. For an "I" to be autonomous in this sense is to have the capacity to become part of a "we".[11] To be a sovereign citizen is to have a certain normative authority to give (universal) laws that bind others (and ourselves), on condition that the laws given can also (potentially) be rationally endorsed by all other members of the community. In Sellarsian terms we can understand the capacity of sovereignty as the capacity to form intentions that commit both ourselves and others, which just is the capacity to form we-intentions.

3 Sellars on the Moral Point of View

Sellars argues that Kantian practical laws should be understood as what he calls categorical we-intentions.[12] This is supposed to capture Kant's thought that practical laws "are valid for the will of every rational being" (KpV, AA 05: 19). For Sellars, claims about obligations are best understood in terms of what he calls the categorical reasonableness of intentions. Thus he argues that the claim that "I ought to do A, if I am in C" is equivalent to the claim that "I shall do A, if I am in C" is categorically reasonable (Sellars, 2023a, 171), and the goal of his project is to offer an account of how an intention can be categorically reasonable. Thus he argues that "The central theme of Kant's ethical theory is, in our terminology, the

---

[11] I think this appeal to the possibility of we-intentions, and the idea of co-sovereignty, helps explain how essentially active autonomous agents can be subject to laws that are partially given by others. Rauscher (2018) expresses a worry about how an active agent can be passive when he writes: "Reason would have to be able to intuit the independent value of humanity as and end in itself in other beings in themselves, in which **case it would have to be passive relative to the value property** and the latter would have to actively effect reason. But **there is no mechanism by which one being in itself can affect another being in itself except through intuition as appearance**, which brings back the point that there is not place in nature for an independent value property. (161 – emphasis added.) Rauscher's account would seem to imply that there can be no real interaction between essentially active intelligible agents, only some form of pre-established harmony. I suggest Kant explains the notion of intelligible interaction in terms of the idea of co-legislation in an ideal republic, where each citizen is both sovereign and subject to the law. For a fuller defense of this claim, see Thorpe (2010). In that paper, I analyze worries like Rauscher's as emerging from what I call the principle of active inherence.

[12] For an excellent overview of Sellars' ethics see Koon (2018).

reasonableness of intentions. In what sense or senses, if any, can intentions be said to be reasonable, i.e. have a claim on the assent of a rational being?" (Sellars, 2023a, 168).

In this section I will briefly explain Sellar's position without attempting to justify each of his claims. His account can be broken down into five distinct claims.

(1) Sellars argues, contra Kant, that moral obligations should be understood in terms of intentions, not imperatives. I think his arguments for this are plausible, for the practice of commanding presupposes a background of obligations. Merely telling someone to do something, even oneself, does not in and of itself create an obligation. So we cannot cash out obligations in terms of tellings. Thus Sellars explains that "although commands, like promises, presuppose principles of obligation, surely, it will be said, simple imperatives do not. Telling someone to do something does not as such appear to create an obligation on his part to do it." (Sellars, 2023b, 373). And "deciding what to do is no more telling ourselves what to do than deciding what is the case is telling ourselves what is the case" (Sellars, 2023a, 148). Giving a command, like making a promise, is a performative, while forming an intention is not. And "whereas promising is a performative which binds the speaker, issuing a command binds the person to whom it is issued. Thus, issuing a command within the limits of one's authority "creates" a presumptive prima-facie obligation to do the action commanded on the part of the person wo whom it is addressed [...]. [T]he claim which commands have on our obedience is but a special case of the claim which our obligations have upon us. Obeying a command, like keeping a promise, is a special case of doing one's duty — though to characterize any particular obeying or promise-keeping as a doing of one's duty is, of course, a defeasible matter." (Sellars 2023b, 372). Hence, we cannot ground our duties, in general, on the idea of a command as determining which commands entail obligations entails the existence of some obligation to obey certain commands.

(2) There are rational relations between intentions, mirroring (theoretical) relations between the contents of our intentions. Thus, Sellars argues,

> An ideally rational being would intend the implications of his intentions, just as he would believe the implications of his beliefs. [...] If 'P' implies 'Q', then it is unreasonable to believe that P is the case without believing that Q is the case. (Though, as noted above, in point of fact one may well believe the former without believing the latter.) Similarly if 'It shall be the case that P' implies 'It shall be the case that Q' [i]t is unreasonable to intend that P be the case without intending that Q be the case. (Though, again, in point of fact one may very well intend the former without intending the latter and may even intend that the latter not be the case.) (Sellars, 2023a, 145)

Thus, if I intend to make dinner tonight but there is no food in the fridge so the only way I can make dinner is if I go shopping, then insofar as I am (ideally) rational I intend to go shopping. This account is meant to explain how one intention can be reasonable relative to another intention, and so explains the "hypothetical" (or as Sellars prefers "relative") reasonableness of intentions. His goal, however, is to show how some intentions can be categorically reasonable, and he thinks that this involves finding a non-derivatively categorically reasonable intention. Thus, Sellars explains:

> It has been easy to assume that relative and categorical reasonableness are incompatible: that an intention can have one or the other, but not both. This assumption is simply false. [...] Implication preserves truth in theoretical arguments. We should explore the possibility that it preserves categorical reasonableness in practical arguments. If so, then, an intention can be categorically reasonable, and yet derivative from another intention — provided, of course, that the latter in turn is categorically reasonable. // Categorical reasonableness must not be confused with intrinsic reasonableness. The confusion between these two has been even more damaging to Kant exegesis than the tendency to suppose that a categorically reasonable intention cannot be conditional in its logical form. On the other hand, even if categorical reasonableness is not the same as intrinsic reasonableness, we are faced with the fact that if there are to be derivative categorically reasonable intentions there must be one or more intentions whose categorical reasonableness is non-derivative or intrinsic. (Sellars, 2023a, 173)

The main task of the final section of *Science and Metaphysics* is to explain the possibility of such a non-derivatively categorical intention.

(3) Sellars distinguishes between "intentions that something be the case" and "intentions to do" (Sellars, 2023a, 174) and this distinction is supposed to ground the distinction between what he calls ought-to-be's and ought-to-do's. And he argues that morality needs to be grounded in an intention that something be the case rather than an intention to do, thus ultimately grounding ought-to-do's in an ought-to-be. It is this prioritizing of an ought-to-be that makes Sellars' Kant interpretation, like Guyer's, essentially teleological. Now, of course intentions to do can be derived from intentions that something be the case. For example, if "I intend that it be the case that p" and the only way it can become the case that p is if I do q, then insofar as I am ideally rational, "I intend to do q."

Now because Sellars thinks that an ought-to-be grounds all of our ought-to-do's, our non-derivatively categorical intention should be thought of as the expression of an intention that something be the case. And given that expressions of ought-to-be's are the expression of what we value,[13] the content of a non-derivatively categorical

---

[13] Sellars (2023a) explains that expressions of individual valuing can be expressed by sentences with the form "I would that...", whereas expressions of valuing from what he calls "the moral point of view" (179) have the form "We would that..." And "to value from a moral point of view is

intention should be thought of as what Guyer, following Kant, calls a universally valid end. Guyer should be sympathetic to this aspect of Sellars' position as it expresses a fundamentally teleological interpretation of Kantian ethics as it places the question of what we value prior to the question of what we ought to do, and as such, for Sellars, claims about what we ought to do are ultimately derivative from claims about what we value.

(4) Sellars thinks that a central aspect of morality is its intersubjective validity, and he thinks this is only possible if moral intentions are ultimately rooted in we-intentions. Sellars argues that a defining aspect of obligations is that one person's claims about obligations can contradict another's, whereas expressions of (individual) intentions can only conflict with one another but cannot logically exclude one another. Thus, Sellars argues that "one person can contradict another person's ought, whereas shalls [intentions] conflict but do not contradict." (Sellars, 2023b, 406). Another way of putting this is "that ought, unlike shall [intend], has a proper negative" (Sellars, 2023b, 406). That is, if Peter thinks that "Martin ought to give all his money to charity", and Martin thinks that "Martin ought not to give all his money to charity", only one of them can be right; the truth of an ought claim logically excludes the truth of its negation. The logic of (individual) intentions is quite different; such claims do not really have external negations. The truth of "Peter intends that Martin give all his money to charity" does not entail the falsity of "Martin does not intend to give all his money to charity".[14] So any attempt to ground obligations in intentions has to explain how expressions of intentions can logically exclude one another. And Sellars' answer is that although the expressions of individual intentions do not have this feature the expressions of we-intentions do. Thus, if Martin claims that "We intend to give all our money to charity" and Peter claims that "We do not intend to give all of our money to charity" only one of them can be right. Thus, Sellars (2023a) argues that, "[t]wo people can affirm the same proposition in a strong sense of 'same'. But as far as the intentions we have so far considered are concerned [i.e. individual intentions], intentions can at best be parallel. They are irreducibly egocentric. ... (176). But this is not the case with "statements in the first-person plural [which] have the interesting properties that

---

to value as a member of the relevant community, which as far as the present argument is concerned, I shall assume to be mankind generally." (Sellars, 2020a, 179.) So the content of an non-derivatively categorical we-intention expresses what we ultimately value from within the moral point of view.

14 One crucial feature of Sellars' account is that we can have intentions concerning not just ourselves but about others too. If Peter intends that it be the case that Martin gives all his money to charity, in so far as he is rational, he will form the intention to do what he can to *persuade* Martin to give all his money to charity.

(a) they express the speakers' intention, yet (b) the intentions expressed are in the strongest sense the same." (177).¹⁵ Such we-intentions have an "intersubjective form" (177). Therefore, Sellars concludes that insofar as we understand ought claims in terms of the expression of intentions, the only candidate for a non-derivatively categorical intention will be some sort of we-intention as only we-intentions have the necessarily intersubjective form.

(5) Having examined the form of any non-derivatively categorical intention Sellars (2023a) next turns to its content. And he unconvincingly argues that the content must involve the maximization of welfare. Thus, he argues,

> the intention "It shall-we be the case that our welfare is maximized" does seem to have an authority which is more than a mere matter of its being generally accepted. It is a conceptual fact that people constitute a community, a we, by virtue of thinking of each other as one of us, and by willing the common good not under the species of benevolence — but by willing it as one of us, or from a moral point of view. (181)¹⁶

And he concludes by explaining that if his argument is correct, then "ethical statements are universal in three dimensions, (a) in their content… (b) in their subjective form (their logical intersubjectivity) We would that… (c) in their objectivity (in that there is, in principle, a decision procedure with respect to specific ethical statements)" (181f).¹⁷

Now, although, I am very sympathetic to Sellars' account of the (necessarily) intersubjective form of moral claims, I think there are good reasons for a Kantian to reject the idea that the underived categorical we-intention should be thought of as involving the commitment to maximizing welfare. For Kant, such a commitment is just not formal enough. And, as Kant argues, the idea of happiness is "an

---

15 Sellars (2023b) expresses a similar point, arguing, "we must distinguish between two shalls, one corresponding to 'We intend… ' and one to 'I, for myself, intend…'. Let us represent them, respectively, as 'shallw' and 'shallI'. *I suggest that ought, as an expression of intention, is a special case of shallw*. There are, in this case, two dimensions to the universality of moral principles as universal intentions: (1) the formal universality, or universality of application which can be represented by the formula, 'All of us shall do A in C'; (2) the universality of the intending itself, which can be represented by modifying the above formula to read, 'All of us shallw do A in C.'" (412).

16 And he makes a similar claim that the content must be understood by appeal to "the general welfare" in Sellars, 2023b, 414.

17 This claim that ethical statements must be universal in both their form and content is a descendent of Rousseau's account of the distinction between a law and a decree, with the argument that laws must be general in (at least) two senses: they must come from all and apply to all. Thus, Rousseau (2002) explains that [w]hen I say that the object of the laws is always general, I mean that the law considers subjects collectively, and actions as abstract, never a man as an individual nor a particular action." (179)

ideal of the imagination, which rests on merely empirical grounds" (GMS, AA 04: 418) not an idea of reason, and so the idea of maximizing it is incoherent. And as Guyer argues:

> Even though happiness seems to be a general concept and all agents appear to agree in striving for it, in fact each agent's conception of happiness is nothing but the conception of the satisfaction of all of her various individual desires, and because of the natural conflicts of desires there are inevitably conflicts within any one individual's conception of happiness as well as among several individuals' conceptions of happiness. Such conflicts prevent the general idea of happiness from serving as a universal and necessary goal and source of practical law. (2000b, 134)

If we want to include some basic value within our most fundamental law, then freedom seems a far more plausible candidate than happiness. Thus, to Guyerize Sellars, we might think that the best candidate for the underived categorical we-intention would be:

(A) We-intend that it be the case that the freedom of each of us (individually) be promoted.

Although another plausible Kantian contender for the content of such an underivatively categorical we-intention involves the idea of a realm of ends. And I think this involves the idea that both the form and the content of such an intention must be expressed in the nominative first person plural; the content must involve a reference to 'we' and not just to 'us'. Thus, as an alternative formulation I suggest:

(B) We-intend that it be the case that we only intend what each of us can intend.

I think this formulation better captures Kant's claim that the moral law be nothing more than "the mere form of a universal law giving" (KpV, AA 05: 27). In addition, it brings the "we" as a collective agent into the content of the moral law rather than just leaving it as part of the form. As such, this formulation stresses the importance of laws in the content of Kant's fundamental principle, for laws must come from all, and so a principle that demands lawlikeness as part of its content has to include some reference to "we" in its content, and not just "us". In addition, this formulation entails a commitment to publicizabiliy and transparency in a way that a commitment to promote overall freedom does not; perhaps the best ways of promoting the freedom of each of us may involve some deception and sometimes interacting with others according to principles that one cannot share with them. I think (B) can also be expressed as:

(C) We-intend that it be the case that we constitute a realm of ends (governed by laws that each of us can endorse).

And such an account of the (universal) content of the moral principle does have an object (or end), namely the idea of a realm of ends, so satisfying Guyer's constraint that all willing (hence all intentions) must have an object, and that our fundamental moral principle must have a universally valid end.

4 How and Why to Take the Moral Point of View

Sellars' account raises two questions: Firstly, how is it possible to take the moral point of view? And secondly, what necessitates us to take this point of view? And my answer to both these questions is that we have and can recognize in others the capacity for autonomy, as the capacity for sovereignty. The first question is answered by the existence of the capacity for sovereignty, the second by the dignity of this capacity.

Let me start by answering the "how" question first. The possibility of taking the moral point of view presupposes a capacity to form-we intentions. And this requires that each potential member of the "we" has the capacity to form we-intentions. But this just is the capacity of autonomy understood as the capacity for sovereignty, as I have defined it, as the capacity to form intentions that bind both myself and others.

The "why" question seems to be more difficult, what Sellars would call a 64,000$ question. For why should we take the moral point of view, and include all human beings within it? Sellars (2023a, 184f) attempts to answer this question, but does not even convince himself. From my perspective there is a sense in which it is very easy to answer this question. To be autonomous just is (from one perspective) to have a certain type of normative power; the power to demand of others that they take the moral point of view and include us with within the domain of their "we". And if asked why we should assume that others are autonomous in this sense, I think we can argue that it should be regarded as something like a postulate of practical reason; morality only makes sense in so far as we take others to have such a normative power and that we have the capacity to recognize which bits of the phenomenal world have this power.[18]

---

[18] For a fuller defense of this appeal to a postulate of practical reason here, see Thorpe (2018).

What it is to be "human" in the moral sense is (by definition) to have the normative power to demand to be included within the scope of the we; it is just analytic that all human beings should be included within the scope of the we of any non-derivatively categorical we-intention. On this account the difficult question is not why all "humans" should be included in the scope of the moral "we", but are there any "humans" and this sense, and if so, how can we recognize them. To which my answer is that in so far as we are committed to morality, we have to pre-suppose that there are "humans" in the morally relevant sense and that we have a reliable capacity to recognize them.[19]

5 The Dignity and Value of Humanity

The argument I have given so far presupposes a distinction between dignity and value. Values are ends to be effected; to value something is to make it an object of one's faculty of desire (or will); To possess dignity, on the other had is to possess a certain type of normative status or power — a being with dignity demands respect. However, the fact that humanity demands respect is compatible with claiming that it is also something of value to be cultivated.

Kant's claim that human beings are ends-in-themselves is to be understood in terms of us possessing a certain type of normative status rather than having unconditional value. In this I agree with Bader (forthcoming) who argues that we need to distinguish between "the axiological property of something that is unconditionally good from the deontological status that something has that possesses dignity" (3)[20] and he argues that "value bearers are ends to be effected [...] yet humanity is a self-standing end" (2) and that "the absolute worth (or dignity) of humanity cannot be a type of unconditional goodness" (3). When Kant claims that humanity is an end-in-itself, Kant is not claiming that humanity is to be understood as unconditionally good, or following Guyer, a universally valid or necessary end. Instead, as Bader argues, dignity plays a "crucial role in Kants ethics by determining the domain over which maxims have to be universalizable" (2). I agree with this as far as it goes. But I think that the dignity of humanity does not merely fix the scope of the moral law — although it does do this. Rather it must be

---

19 For a reading which argues that it is a moral responsibility to presuppose that each moral agent is a co-contributor to all our "we-intentions" with respect to the highest good see Tilev (2022), esp. section 4.
20 Although, I do see why we need to call this status "deontological".

understood as a normative power, as a capacity to (normatively) demand to be included in the scope of the moral law, to be included as one of us, who are able to form-we intentions.

I think I disagree with Bader, however, on two points. Firstly, I am more sympathetic to teleological readings of Kant and the fact that humanity (understood in one way) has dignity is compatible with the claim that humanity (perhaps in another sense) has value. Thus, I think that, for Kant, human beings have dignity as beings with the capacity for sovereignty and hence demand to be included within the scope of the moral law. But this claim is compatible with Guyer's claim that human beings [also] have unconditional value as beings with the capacity to set (and pursue) ends, and that the promotion of this capacity is a universally valid end. We just shouldn't confuse the notion of being an end-in-itself with that of being a universally valid end.

Secondly, I agree with Bader that humanity is the ground of obligation and sets the scope of the domain of universalization, but not merely because if no humans existed the domain would be empty. We should think of humanity not merely as a moral predisposition, but also as a normative power. There are various ways to think about this power. We can think of it as the capacity to interact with others on the basis of mutual respect. Following the psychologist Gibson, we can think of being human in this sense in terms of possessing a particular social affordance.[21] Or we can think of it as the power to give law that can bind both oneself and others. Or we can think of it as a capacity to form we-intentions. Either way, being human involves the capacity to make moral demands on others and to be able to recognize such demands from others, and as such we should think of humanity in this sense as a normative power. Being human entails the capacity to recognize humanity and recognizing humanity involves recognizing a (potential) source of obligation. So having dignity is not merely having a certain normative status.

6 Conclusion

I have argued that we can make claims about the value of freedom and the dignity of autonomy compatible by suggesting that we can understand the value of freedom as central to the content of the moral point of view, whereas the dignity of

---

[21] See Thorpe (2018) for an account of how we can understand humanity as a capacity for sovereignty in broadly naturalistic terms as a social affordance.

autonomy is what necessitates us to take the moral point of view. However, claiming the two positions are compatible does not entail that we should combine them, for perhaps there is a more plausible Kantian account of the content of an underived categorical we-intention. And I have suggested that Kant regards the idea of a realm of ends as a universally valid end and this is a more plausible Kantian candidate for the content of an underived categorically valid we-intention than either the idea of freedom understood at the capacity to set ends (as Guyer suggests) or universal welfare (as Sellar suggests).

References

Bader, Ralf (forthcoming). "The Dignity of Humanity." In *Rethinking the Value of Humanity*, ed. by Sarah Buss and Nandi Theunissen. Oxford.
Broad, C. D. (1930). *Five Types of Ethical Theory*, London.
Guyer, Paul (2000a). "Freedom as the Inner Value of the World." In *Kant on Freedom, Law and Happiness*, Cambridge, 96–125.
Guyer, Paul (2000b). "Kant's Morality of Law and Morality of Freedom." In *Kant on Freedom, Law and Happiness*, Cambridge, 129–171.
Guyer, Paul (2005a). "Kant on the Theory and Practice of Autonomy". In *Kant's System of Nature and Freedom*, Oxford, 115–145.
Guyer, Paul (2005b). "Ends of Reason and Ends of Nature: The Place of teleology in Kant's Ethics." In *Kant's System of Nature and Freedom*, Oxford, 169–197.
Guyer, Paul (2005c). "The Form and Matter of the Categorical Imperative." In *Kant's System of Nature and Freedom*, Oxford, 146–168.
Guyer, Paul (2005d). "Deductions of the Principles of Right." In *Kant's System of Nature and Freedom*, Oxford, 198–242.
Guyer, Paul (2005e). "Kant's System of Duties." In *Kant's System of Nature and Freedom*, Oxford, 243–272.
Guyer, Paul (2005f). "Purpose in Nature." In *Kant's System of Nature and Freedom*, Oxford, 343–371.
Guyer, Paul (2016a). "Kantian Perfectionism." In *The Values of Freedom*, Oxford, 70–86.
Guyer, Paul (2016b). "Freedom and the Essential Ends of Humankind." In *The Values of Freedom*, Oxford, 54–69.
Guyer, Paul (2016c). "Setting and Pursuing Ends: Internal and External Freedom." In *The Values of Freedom*, Oxford, 87–104.
Guyer, Paul (2016d). "Kant, Autonomy and Modernity." In *The Values of Freedom*, Oxford, 3–20.
Guyer, Paul (2016e). "Freedom, Ends and Duties in *Vigilantius*." In *The Values of Freedom*, Oxford, 105–125.
Guyer, Paul (2016f). "The Proof Structure of the *Groundwork*." In *The Values of Freedom*, Oxford, 127–145.
Guyer, Paul (2016g). "A Passion for Reason." In *The Values of Freedom*, Oxford, 201–215.
Koons, Jeremy Randel (2018). *The Ethics of Wilfrid Sellars*, Routledge.
Louden, Robert B. (1998). "Toward a Genealogy of 'Deontology'." *Journal of the History of Philosophy* 34 (4), 571–592.
Phillips, David (2019). *Rossian Ethics: W. D. Ross and Contemporary Moral Theory*, Oxford.
Rousseau, J. J (2002). *The Social Contract and The First and Second Discourses*, ed. by Susan Dunn, Yale.

Sellars, Wilfred (2023a). "Objectivity, Intersubjectivity and the Moral Point of View [chapter six of Science and Metaphysics]." In *The metaphysics of practice: writings on action, community, and obligation*, ed. by Kyle Ferguson and Jeremy Randel Koons, Oxford, 138–187.
Sellars, Wilfred (2023b). "Imperatives, Intentions and the Logic of 'Ought'." In *The metaphysics of practice: writings on action, community, and obligation*, ed. by Kyle Ferguson and Jeremy Randel Koons, Oxford, 367–420.
Thorpe, Lucas (2010). "Is Kant's Realm of Ends a Unum per Se? Aquinas, Suárez, Leibniz and Kant on Composition." *British Journal of the History of Philosophy* 18 (3), 461–485.
Thorpe, Lucas (2011). "Autonomy and Community." In *Kant and the Concept of Community* [A North American Kant Society Special Volume], ed. by Lucas Thorpe and Charlton Payne, Rochester.
Thorpe, Lucas (2013). "One Community or Many? Community and Interaction in Kant: From Logic to Politics via Metaphysics and Ethics." In *Politics and Metaphysics in Kant*, ed. by Howard Williams, Sorin Baiasu and Sami Pihlström, Cardiff.
Thorpe, Lucas (2018). "Kant, Guyer and Tomasello on the Capacity to Recognize the Humanity of Others." In *Kant on Freedom and Spontaneity*, ed. by Kate Moran, Cambridge.
Thorpe, Lucas (2019). "What's wrong with Constructivist Readings of Kant?" In *The Philosophy of Kant*, ed. by Ricardo Gutiérrez Aguilar, New York.
Tilev, Seniye (2022). "What should we hope?" *Philosophia* 50 (5), 2685–2706.
Vatansever, Saniye (2021). "Kant's Coherent Theory of the Highest Good", *International Journal for Philosophy of Religion* 89 (3), 263–283.

Julian Wuerth
Guyer, the Grounding of Kant's Categorical Imperative, and the Elimination of Sensibility Procedure

Abstract: Paul Guyer interprets Kant's ethics as teleological, with humanity as the ultimate end. On this interpretation, Kant's Formula of Universal Law (FUL) on its own amounts to blind obedience to law. To make sense and to motivate, FUL must instead be interpreted as mandatory solely as a means to human freedom as spelled out in the Formula of Humanity (FH), so that FUL *rests on* FH. The current essay, however, identifies a *common* argument for *independent* FH and FUL formulations of the categorical imperative in what is termed Kant's Elimination of Sensibility Procedure (ESP). Kant's critical philosophy distinguishes in kind between sensibility and understanding, and Kant now uses this distinction to avoid the mistake that in his view has doomed every previous ethics: conflating the pragmatic and the moral. By systematically isolating the moral through ESP, Kant can finally clarify the form (FUL) and matter (FH) of the categorical imperative.

Keywords: categorical imperative, universal law, humanity

At the conference held at Brown University in honor of Paul Guyer on the occasion of his retirement from teaching, Reed Winegar asked Paul which single question he would ask Kant were Kant to return from the dead. Ignoring Fred Rauscher's sensible suggestion, "How did you return from the dead?," Paul, after some reflection, answered "What is the foundation of morality?" Three hundred years after Kant's birth and two hundred and twenty years after his death, Kant's exact answer remains enigmatic, even for arguably the greatest Kant scholar ever, and even though Kant arguably took the question of morality, "What should I do?," to be the most important question in philosophy. A year ago, in an email to me, Paul summarized his interpretation of Kant's answer to this question as I worked on my own for a forthcoming book, and he added that he looked forward to seeing my own interpretation — "even, or especially, if you differ from me!" This invitation to disagree with him captures much of the generous spirit with which Paul approaches philosophy and approached his role, decades ago, as my dissertation advisor. Much to his credit,

Paul was never interested in producing replicas of himself, much less disciples, but instead partners in philosophical inquiry and scholarship. In what follows,
I accept Paul's invitation, offering an interpretation that differs from his, even if there is much on which we agree. It is a pleasure and an honor to do so on this special occasion, made possible by *Kant-Studien*,[1] of honoring Paul for a lifetime (that is not over yet!) of exceptional achievement, on this three hundredth anniversary of the birth of Immanuel Kant.

I start with a review of Guyer's interpretation of Kant's criticism of the rationalist perfectionist tradition in ethics. As Guyer characterizes it, rationalist perfectionism falls short for Kant because it is purely formal, a problem Kant fixes by introducing into his own ethics a matter, or a good, on which to ground moral obligation. As Guyer understands it, this ultimate matter or good is for Kant humanity, which for Guyer boils down to freedom, and this is presented by Kant in his second formulation of the categorical imperative, the Formula of Humanity as an End-in-Itself (FH). On Guyer's interpretation, Kant's first formulation of the categorical imperative, his Formula of Universal Law (FUL), is by contrast with FH, and like the rationalist perfectionists' moral law, formal and empty. Obedience to FUL, without reference to FH, would for Guyer accordingly be "blind obedience" to law. It is only if and when we hitch FUL to FH, showing that the universalizability of maxims is a necessary precondition for respecting and promoting the matter, or content, of humanity, or freedom, that FUL gets off the ground with any justification: in Guyer's words in *Kant on Freedom, Law, and Happiness*[2], "obedience to universal law [is] mandatory solely as the necessary condition for the realization of human freedom" (KFLH, 1).

Guyer, as usual, musters strong textual evidence for his interpretation of Kant's views on both the rationalist perfectionist position and the relationship of the FUL to the FH, and I do not hope to refute his interpretation but instead, at best, provide a plausible alternative. I should also add that, while I provide a partial defense of the *foundations* of FUL, I believe that Kant's own formulation of FUL is highly problematic, especially its "contradiction in conception" test. My argument draws on an interpretation I have developed elsewhere[3] of a single basic underlying procedure across Kant's various arguments for the categorical imperative, grounded in my

---

[1] Many thanks to Konstantin Pollok and Margit Ruffing for their fine editorial work on this volume.
[2] Paul Guyer, *Kant on Freedom, Law, and Happiness*. Cambridge: Cambridge University Press, 2000. Hereafter "KFLH."
[3] Julian Wuerth, "Categorical Imperative," in *The Cambridge Kant Lexicon*, ed. by Julian Wuerth (Cambridge, Cambridge University Press, 2021), 67–94; and Julian Wuerth, *Kant on Mind, Action, and Ethics* (Oxford: Oxford University Press, 2014).

interpretation of Kant's account of our mental faculties and theory of action, which I call Kant's Elimination of Sensibility Procedure, or ESP. I have argued that Kant views the history of ethics before him as united in its conflation of intellectual and sensible sources of the moral law and as thus united in its mixing together "in proportions unknown" of moral and pragmatic considerations, spoiling all efforts to identify a properly *moral* law. The rationalists, in particular, intellectualize sensibility, while the empiricists sensualize the intellect. Operating against the backdrop of his distinction in kind between sensibility and understanding, Kant's strategy with ESP is to systematically eliminate as inadequate all offerings of sensibility: our sensible feelings, our sensible desires, the objects of our sensible inclinations, and also our sensible cognitions of various moral codes in practice. Kant rejects these offerings of sensibility for a reason: they are not up to the demands of a categorical imperative or a good will determined by it. In this essay, I add to my ESP argument a new historical piece. I look first at some of Kant's views in the early 1760s and then at how Kant's ethics transitioned away from moral sense theory in 1769 with the advent of his distinction in kind between sensibility and understanding. At this point Kant gave up on his attempts to accommodate the categorical nature of moral imperatives within a moral sense theory, and he turned instead to an ethics of reason. Next, I argue that Kant was rejecting rationalist perfectionism in good part because of its failure to draw the distinction in kind between sensibility and understanding, which meant that its concept of perfection did not even limit itself to the intellectual but instead gestured vaguely toward an undifferentiated combination of moral and pragmatic goods. Kant, by contrast, starting from our shared understanding of either the value of a good will or the nature of a moral law as a categorical imperative for us, uses ESP to systematically reject sensibility and isolate pure practical reason, and this argument yields FUL. On my interpretation, then, one does not need to rest FUL on FH.

1 Guyer on Kant's Rejection of Rationalist Perfectionism and the Dependence of FUL on FH

Paul Guyer has written extensively in defense of his view that Kant's ethics is a form of teleology, whose telos, goal, end, or matter, is humanity, freedom, or autonomy — Guyer tends to use these terms interchangeably. This matter is what Kant presents in the second formulation of his categorical imperative, his famous Formula of Humanity as an End in Itself (FH). As Guyer sees it, Kant's first formulation of the categorical imperative, his equally famous Formula of Universal Law, which specifies the *form* of morally permissible willing, is not an equal partner alongside the second formulation of the categorical imperative; if taken on its own, the first formulation would be left to insist upon "obedience to law for its own sake," or "blind obedience to law," and it avoids this fate only to the extent it is hitched to the second formulation as a means to the end set out in this second formulation, demanding universalizability of maxims merely as the necessary condition for satisfying the demands of the second formulation that we respect and promote humanity/freedom in ourselves and others. In the Introduction to his *Kant on Freedom, Law, and Happiness*, Guyer lays out his impressively bold thesis:

> Yet Kant has also seemed to many to advocate an insistence upon obedience to law for its own sake, an insistence upon blind obedience to law that in the twentieth century just ended has been associated with the destruction of everything for which the Enlightenment stood. A profound paradox can be avoided only if it can be shown that Kant intended obedience to universal law to be mandatory solely as the necessary condition for the realization of human freedom and through that freedom a systematic and unselfish distribution of happiness among all persons seeking a systematic union of their purposes in a world both natural and moral in which each and every person is treated as an end and never merely as a means. On this account, while all human beings must be treated as ends in themselves, the sheer fact of adherence to universal law is not an end in itself but is rather the means to the realization of the human potential for autonomy or freedom in both choice and action. (KFLH, 1)

Guyer's interpretation of Kant's ethics sees important seeds for Kant's mature ethics in Kant's 1764 *Inquiry Concerning the Distinctness of the Principles of Natural Theology and Morality*, otherwise known as his "Prize Essay" — even though Moses Mendelssohn won the actual monetary prize while Kant merely had his essay published along with Mendelssohn's as a consolation prize of sorts. In that essay, Kant, who at the time was still a moral sense theorist, faulted rationalist perfectionism, as practiced by Wolff and Baumgarten, for offering a purely formal ethics that was empty, pointing out that when regarded on their own, "no specifically determinate obligation flows from [the rationalist perfectionists'] two rules of the good" (UD, AA 02: 299). These two rules of good tell us to "perform the most perfect action in your power" and "abstain from doing that which will hinder the realization of the greatest possible perfection" (UD, AA 02: 299). But while useless on their own, these formal rules can be rendered useful — if, and only if, Kant tells us, they are "combined with indemonstrable material principles of practical cognition" (ibid.). At the time, as a moral sense theorist, Kant saw this material being supplied by our "unanalyzable feeling of the good" (ibid.). Surveying this material, Guyer identifies in it a two-part lesson that Kant takes to heart and never surrenders, namely, that a formal law is useless on its own and that a formal law must ultimately rely on a material law: "the key insight for Kant's eventual practical philosophy contained in this work is then the idea that [i] moral philosophy too must begin with a fundamental though indemonstrable material or substantive principle, a fundamental source of value, and [ii] cannot rely on any purely formal law alone (KFLH, 8; see also 41f). I will return to the *Inquiry* later to suggest other lessons Kant takes from it for use in his mature ethics.

Of course, if Guyer wants to defend an interpretation of Kant's moral philosophy as recognizing a moral matter or moral end toward which moral choice needs to be responsive, he will need to defend himself against the inevitable objection that Kant's ethics is deontological, not teleological. Guyer does exactly this, examining Kant's well-known discussion in his 1788 *Critique of Practical Reason* in which he asserts what is often taken for the textbook definition of deontology, that the right must come before the good. As Guyer makes clear, however, Kant's point is *not* that the moral right has to come before a *moral good* but only that the moral right must come before, or be the condition under which we pursue, the good understood as the *empirical, pragmatic good, of our happiness*. As long as the sought-after unconditionally-valuable good is found, which would require that we go outside of the conditioned empirical realm, Kant's concern about the good coming before the right would be addressed and the good would *not* need to come after the right. Guyer (KFLH, 132f) quotes Kant on this point:

> The concept of the good as of an object does not determine and make possible the moral law, but on the contrary the moral law first determines and makes possible the concept of the good insofar as it deserves this name.
>
> This remark, which concerns merely the method of the highest moral inquiries, is of importance. It explains at once the ground responsible for all confusion of philosophers in regard to the highest principles of morals. For they sought for an object of the will in order to make it into the matter and ground of a law (which would then be the determining ground of the will not immediately but only mediately through the object that is brought to the feeling of pleasure or displeasure), when they should have first sought for a law that would determine the will immediately and an object only in accordance with this law. Now whether they placed this object of pleasure, which was to yield the highest concept of the good, in happiness, in perfection, in moral feeling, or in the will of God, their principle was always heteronomy, and they must unavoidably have stumbled into empirical conditions for a moral law (KpV 5:64).

I agree with Guyer fully on this point: Kant is by no means opposed to a "good" understood as an "end," or a "matter," *per se*, serving as the goal of a moral imperative; he is instead opposed only to having an *empirical* good, end, or matter, rooted in incentives and the goal of happiness, serve as the goal of a moral imperative. We see the same point made by Kant in the *Groundwork*, in so many words, when he also addresses what he later cites in the *Critique of Practical Reason* as "the ground responsible for all confusion of philosophers in regard to the highest principles of morals":

> When we look back upon all previous attempts that have been made to discover the principle of morality, there is no reason now to wonder why they one and all had to fail [...]. For when man is thought as being merely subject to a law (whatever it might be), then the law had to carry with it some interest functioning as an attracting stimulus or as a constraining force for obedience [...] duty was never discovered, but only the necessity of acting from a certain interest [...] [so that] the imperative had to be always conditional and could never possibly serve as a moral command. (GMS 04: 432f)

Here Kant makes the same point, namely, that all previous moral philosophies have failed, and he explains that they have failed because they have not identified a law of *pure practical reason*, which *we* ourselves recognize as valid; instead, previous moral philosophies have understood us to be subject to laws imposed from *without*. This relates to the point in the cited passage from the *Critique of Practical Reason* because, as Kant here explains, if we do not ourselves recognize the validity of a moral imperative, we will only subject ourselves to it from a "certain interest," i.e., *on the basis of our subjective empirical incentives, and so with an eye toward our own happiness*. Not surprisingly, then, and consistent with Guyer's point, when Kant searches, in the *Groundwork*, for an end with absolute value that could serve as the end set out by a moral law, he accordingly specifically rejects "*subjective* ends, which rest on incentives" (GMS, AA 04: 427, emphasis added), while embracing "*objective* ends [or "matter" GMA, AA 04: 436], which depend on motives valid for every rational being" (GMS, AA 04: 427, emphasis added). Humanity is this objective end, or matter, that depends on motives valid for every rational being. Because "practical principles are formal when they abstract from all subjective ends," but "material [...] when they are founded upon subjective ends" (GMS, AA 04: 427), and because the Formula of Humanity abstracts from all *subjective* ends, it follows that, even though the Formula of Humanity supplies the *objective* end, or matter, for the categorical imperative, it is nonetheless in the sense here described, a "formal" practical principle consistent with Kant's rejection of material ethics.

As Guyer sees it, Kant's presentation of the Formula of Humanity, with its objective end, or matter, is therefore the moment where Kant comes full circle from his discussion in the *Inquiry*. There Kant argued that the rationalist perfectionists' formal principles were empty without combination with "material principles" (UD, AA 02: 299), and now, Guyer argues, Kant has found an end, or matter, in which to ground his mature moral principle and give it content, in effect supplying the Formula of Universal Law with the content it needs.

A few more details need to be reviewed regarding Guyer's account, however. First, when Guyer speaks of the end, matter, or source of value in Kant's ethics, he tends to cluster a number of closely related concepts, namely, those of humanity, freedom, autonomy, and good will. I do not have space here to properly defend a position on the rich question of the relation of these four concepts, but I will say a few things. First, humanity, as the combination of the higher faculties of cognition, feeling, and desire that together constitute rational nature in humans and allow us to set ends for ourselves, is for Kant free, and so humanity also entails the *capacity* for a good will and autonomy, even if we can never know for certain whether someone (even ourselves) has ever had a good will (e.g., GMS, AA 04: 407; V-Anth/Collins, AA 25: 24; MS, AA 06: 447). It is this capacity, specifically, for a good will that comprises the worth of humanity, so that without this capacity we would lose our worth and descend to the rank of mere animality. In the *Metaphysics of Morals*, Kant explains that if we ceased to have moral feeling, which is what "make[s] us aware of the constraint present in the thought of duty," we would become "morally dead," and "then humanity would dissolve (by chemical laws, as it were) into mere animality" (MS, AA 06: 399–400). Here we would not strictly be reduced to animality, because animality, as defined by Kant, lacks self-consciousness, which we would here retain along with any number of our higher faculties. But we would be *like* animality in one key regard, in that we would now lack the capacity to act out of respect for the moral law, and so we would now, like animals (defined by Kant not biologically, but simply as beings lacking self-consciousness and so lacking the capacity for morality) lose all *worth in ourselves*. Kant explains this point in the *Critique of Practical Reason*, making clear that even if we retain the capacity for setting ends for ourselves and the capacity for using reason in the process of setting ends for ourselves, we would still lose all value if we could use reason only *instrumentally*, as a "slave of the passions," to use Hume's words, to pursue happiness alone and not the higher purpose of morality: "That he has reason does not in the least raise [a human] in worth above mere animality if reason only serves the purposes which, among animals, are taken care of by instinct; if this were so, reason would be only a specific way nature had made use of to equip man for the same purpose for which animals are qualified, without fitting him for any higher purpose" (KpV, AA 05: 61). So the good will is at the center of Kant's account of value, being something he and everyone else, in his view, recognizes as self-evidently valuable without qualification, while we likewise all recognize the value in itself of humanity insofar as we recognize it to be a capacity to set ends and have a good will. Here are some supporting quotations, first from his lectures on ethics from the year of the *Groundwork's* publication, in which he repeats his famous claims in the *Groundwork* about a good will: "a good will is simply good without restriction, for itself alone, in every respect and under all circumstances. It is the only thing good without other conditions" (V-Mo/Mron II, AA 29: 599). As Kant explains in the *Groundwork*, it is because humanity is capable of morality that it can have value in itself, or "dignity": "morality is the condition under which alone a rational being can be an end in himself [...]. Hence morality and humanity, insofar as it is capable of morality, alone have dignity"

(GMS, AA 04: 435). So, as I have very briefly argued, while the concepts of humanity and a good will are closely related, a good will is the only thing with unqualified value in itself, while humanity also has value (but not unqualified value, given its capacity for moral failure) in itself, *because* it has the *capacity* for morally worthy choice. At the end of the day, I am not sure whether this interpretation squares with Guyer's.

Next, and importantly, Guyer argues not only that Kant recognizes a matter, end, or telos of sorts — again, he refers mostly to freedom, though also to humanity, autonomy, and good will — but also that the Formula of Universal Law *relies on* the Formula of Humanity and its specified end to "give any rational being a reason to adhere to the principle of morality" (KFLH, 145). In other words, when it comes to the Formula of Universal Law, with its demand that we act on universalizable maxims, there is nothing to *"possibly motivate us to act on the basis of such a law,"* Guyer suggests, unless we rest FUL on FH and the value of humanity, or freedom. Accordingly, we ought to act on universalizable maxims (per FUL) *because* this is how we respect and promote humanity (per FH), so that FUL acquires normative authority only to the extent it is now recognized to specify the means (universalizable maxims) to the end laid out in FH, of respecting and promoting humanity.

2 An Alternative Approach: Kant's Rejection of Rationalist Perfectionism and the Grounding of FUL through the Elimination of Sensibility Procedure

I've now briefly sketched Guyer's interpretation of Kant's views on how form and matter work together in his ethics. Guyer sees Kant rejecting rationalist perfectionism in his 1764 *Inquiry* as formal and empty and proposing a solution to this problem with the introduction of matter into this rationalist perfectionist account — at this early point in Kant's development, the matter contributed by moral feeling. Guyer sees echoes of this strategy in Kant's *Groundwork*, arguing that Kant again views his formal Formula of Universal Law as incomplete, providing no reason or motivation for acting morally, and that it is only the second formulation of the categorical imperative that offers this basis and motivation for the moral law with its account of the matter, or end, of humanity. What I now propose is an alternative narrative spanning the same period considered by Guyer, from the *Inquiry* to the *Groundwork*. While this alternative opposes Guyer's view that there is no reason or motivation to act on FUL without appeal to FH, it may well be compatible with Guyer's interpretation in most other regards.

As Guyer says, Kant's 1764 *Inquiry* criticizes the rationalist perfectionists for presenting a purely formal account that offers no results on its own, and Kant later repeats this criticism of the rationalist perfectionists in many other places, adding that matter needs to be introduced for this perfectionist account to yield results. But there is another criticism that Kant offers of rationalist perfectionism that he will continue to offer throughout his critical philosophy as part of his most sweeping criticism of all previous ethics. This is the criticism that we saw Kant making, above, in the *Groundwork* (GMS, AA 04: 432f) and the *Critique of Practical Reason* (KpV, AA 05: 64): that all systems of ethics prior to Kant failed because they did not properly distinguish, in kind, between the moral and the pragmatic, because they did not properly distinguish, in kind, between sensibility and understanding.

We can see the crude beginnings of this criticism of the rationalists' conflation of the moral and pragmatic in a source from the same year as Kant's *Inquiry*, namely, his 1763–64 *Lectures on Ethics Herder*, and in the *Inquiry* we find additional seeds for Kant's eventual, deeper criticism of the rationalists' conflation of the moral and the pragmatic rooted in Kant's later, mature distinction in kind between sensibility and understanding. First, after Kant introduces a distinction between moral feeling and practical feeling in his 1763–64 *Lectures on Ethics Herder*, he attacks Baumgarten and Wolff for failing to recognize the distinction between moral and practical perfection within their perfectionism: "this distinction is bungled by Baumgarten [...] though everything he says may make for great practical perfection, it does not constitute moral perfection. The latter he omits to define, according to the taste of Wolff, which continually based perfection on the relation between cause and effect, and thus treated it as a means to ends grounded in desire and aversion" (V-PP/Herder, AA 27: 16). While Kant here frames the distinction between the moral and the practical within his merely pre-critical moral sense theory — following the moral sense theorists in their distinction between "self-interested feeling" (V-PP/Herder, AA 27: 03) and (against the "selfish-theorists" such as Hobbes) an additional, "disinterested," or "noble" moral feeling (ibid.) — Kant nonetheless has managed to introduce an important theme that will remain a fixture throughout his later, critical thought: the view that the perfectionists and all other philosophers have failed to properly distinguish the moral from the pragmatic. Moving to Kant's 1764 *Inquiry*, we see Kant for the first time drawing his famous distinction between hypothetical and categorical imperatives, though the terminology differs: "Now, every *ought* expresses a necessity of the action and is capable of two meanings. To be specific: either I ought to do something (as a *means*) if I want something else (as an *end*), or I ought *immediately* to do something else (as an *end*) and make it actual. The former may be called the necessity of the means (*necessitas problematica*), and the latter the necessity of the ends (*necessitas legalis*)" (UD, AA 02: 298). Kant then tells us that "the first kind does not indicate any obligation at all" and then adds — to support Guyer's point about the need for an end in itself — that "They cannot be called obligations as long as they are not subordinated to an end which is necessary in itself" (UD, AA 02: 298f). Kant has now juxtaposed, within his moral sense theory, the distinction, on one hand, between "self-interested feeling" and the "noble" (moral) feeling, and, on the other hand, the distinction between hypothetical and categorical imperatives. The problem is that talk of categorical imperatives, or imperatives that rest on "an end which is necessary in itself" (UD, AA 02: 298), is incompatible with Kant's view expressed in the same source, in keeping with the views of Hume, that our "feeling of the good" never provides insight into "a thing absolutely but only relatively to a being endowed with sensibility" (UD, AA 02: 299). In other words, *moral* imperatives are supposed to be unique in speaking of an end that is necessary *in itself*, while our moral feeling can register value only *relatively*, subject to the nature of our sensibility. In other sources from the 1760s, Kant does make attempts to square the subjective nature of moral feeling with the need to identify an end that is "necessary in itself," following Rousseau in arguing for the special, universal, and even "unerring" nature of *some* of our feelings, namely those that are *natural* moral feelings rather than those feelings corrupted by *custom*: "My reason can err; my moral feeling, only when I uphold custom before natural feeling" (V-PP/Herder, 27: 06). But whether Kant was really convinced even at this stage that feelings could identify ends necessary in themselves is unclear, especially when one considers that, a mere page after writing about moral feeling and ends that are necessary in themselves in the *Inquiry*, Kant concludes the work with a *question* of whether feeling or cognition determines the first principles of practical philosophy (UD, AA 02: 300). In sum, at this point in the early 1760s, Kant is already faulting the rational perfectionists for not adequately distinguishing between moral and pragmatic imperatives, and his first talk about a categorical moral imperative and ends that are recognized as necessary in themselves hints at an even deeper divide to come between the moral and the pragmatic, where reason, and not moral feeling, achieves insight into the moral imperative.

To make a long story short, Kant's switch away from a moral sense theory grounded in sensibility to an ethics of reason happens in 1769–70, with his critical turn to a distinction-in-kind between sensibility and understanding in his 1770 *Inaugural Dissertation* and various *Reflexionen*. In a *Reflexion* from 1772, Kant explains the modal challenge: "The whole difficulty in the dispute over the *principium* of morality is: how is it possible to have a categorical *imperativus*, which is not conditional, under neither problematic nor apodictic conditions (of skill, prudence)"

(R 6725, Refl, AA 19: 141 [1772]). In another *Reflexion* likely from the same year, Kant argues that the moral law's modal status as necessary rules out moral sense as its possible source: "If such a moral sense were possible, then necessary, categorical, and universal laws could not be grounded on it" (R 6754, Refl, AA 19: 149 [1772?]). In a *Reflexion* from 1769–70, Kant explicitly rejects Hutcheson's moral sense theory: "Hutcheson's principle is unphilosophical, because it introduces a new feeling as a ground of explanation, and second *because it sees objective grounds in the laws of sensibility*" (R 6634, Refl, AA 19: 120 [1769–70]). And in the same 1769–70 period, Kant makes clear that he now views *reason* as the source of moral imperatives: "morality is an objective subordination of the will under the motivating grounds of reason" (R 6610, Refl, AA 19: 107 [1769–70]).

And now we return to the rationalist perfectionists. In addition to rejecting moral sense theory once and for all, Kant now, in the *Inaugural Dissertation*, also rejects the rationalist perfectionists. And while he will continue to fault them for offering an empty formalism, his main focus here is on their failure to appropriately distinguish between the moral and the pragmatic. In his earlier *Lectures on Ethics Herder*, we saw Kant level the same basic criticism, but now this failure is due also to the rationalists' failure to draw a distinction in kind between understanding and sensibility. Rather than view the distinction between sensibility and understanding as a distinction in kind, they view it as a distinction merely in degree of logical distinctness: "the sensitive is poorly defined as that which is *more confusedly* cognized, and that which belongs to the understanding as that of which there is a *distinct* cognition. For these are only logical distinctions which *do not touch* at all the things *given*, which underlie every logical comparison. Thus, sensitive representations can be very distinct and representations which belong to the understanding can be extremely confused" (UD, AA 02: 394), Kant explains. Indeed, in Kant's view, were logical distinctness the criterion for determining what is sensible rather than intellectual, the line might even be drawn in the wrong place altogether, given that some sensible cognitions are more distinct than intellectual ones. In order to draw this line in the right place, one needs to instead consider the point of *origin* of these objects of cognition. Here Kant makes this point, faulting Wolff in particular. What's more, he now draws the connection to his ethics, underscoring the crucial role that this distinction plays there:

> Each and every one of these cognitions preserves the sign of its ancestry, so that those belonging to the first group [sensibility], however distinct they be, are called sensitive because of their origin, while those belonging to the second group continue to belong to the understanding, even though they are confused. **Such, for example, is the case with *moral* concepts, which are cognized not by experiencing them but by the pure understanding itself**. But I am afraid it may be that the illustrious WOLFF has, by this distinction between what is sensitive and what belongs to the understanding, a distinction which for him is only logical,

completely abolished, to the great detriment of philosophy, the noblest of the enterprises of antiquity, the discussion of the *character of phenomena and noumena*, and has turned men's minds away from that enquiry to things which are often only logical minutiae (UD, AA 02: 395, boldface added).

In the later (1781/87) *Critique of Pure Reason*, Kant famously criticizes both the rationalists and the empiricists for failing to draw a distinction in kind between sensibility and understanding, with the result that "Leibniz **intellectualized** the appearances, just as Locke **sensitivized** the concepts of the understanding" (KrV, A 271/B 327), and what we have seen here in the moral realm with Kant's assessment of the moral sense theorists and Wolff is the same point: on the empiricist end, the moral sense theorists, including the early Kant himself, sensualized the intellect, understanding reason's moral law to be a form of moral sense; on the rationalist end, Wolff intellectualizes sensibility, not properly isolating understanding and its unique moral law from sensibility because he construes the distinction as one in logical distinctness only. Neither the rationalists nor the empiricists will accordingly be able to properly isolate the intellectual from the sensible and in turn the moral from the pragmatic. The result will be that neither will isolate what Kant will understand to be the unique voice of pure practical reason, and as a result both will fail.

Here Kant's challenge is accordingly not the skeptic, we will see. Kant instead thinks that we all know the moral law, even if this moral law is not always clear. And Kant also thinks we all accept its authority, even if we do try to free ourselves from its specific demands through a process of rationalizing that Kant refers to as the "natural dialectic" (GMS, AA 04: 405). In defense of Kant's optimism about our recognition of a moral law, it can be noted that even Hume kicks off his *Enquiry Concerning the Principles of Morals* by asserting on the first page that it is only "disingenuous disputants" who have ever "denied the reality of moral distinctions," and that it is not conceivable "that any human creature could ever seriously believe that all characters and actions were alike entitled to the affection and regard of every one." Instead, Kant's challenge will be to confront the ubiquitous failure amongst his predecessors and peers to draw a distinction in kind between sensibility and understanding, a failure manifesting itself in the conflation of the moral and the pragmatic. Kant's resulting strategy? With an eye to this distinction in kind, as well as to other sub-faculties of sensibility and understanding, Kant will focus his readers on the unique unconditioned, categorical nature of moral imperatives and the unique unconditioned and unqualified good of a will determined out of respect for the moral law. With his readers focused on these unique, unconditioned features of the moral law and action on it, Kant will then be able to guide them through a systematic, not haphazard, rejection of sensibility as the possible source of the moral law. Having thus isolated pure practical reason, Kant will finally be positioned to clarify the nature of its moral law. This is the argumentative strategy that Kant uses across his mature ethics, which I refer to as Kant's Elimination of Sensibility Procedure. It is a process that Kant also likened to chemistry in his *Critique of Practical Reason*, where he tells us that we should, in approaching moral judgments, adopt "a process similar to that of chemistry, i.e., we may, in repeated experiments on common sense, separate the empirical from the rational, exhibit each of them in a pure state, and show what each by itself can accomplish" (KpV, AA 05: 163; cf. GMS, AA 04: 388f). In taking his readers through this process whereby they first reject sensibility, Kant will in effect have his readers recapitulate his own evolution in ethics.

If we jump ahead from 1769 to the mid-1770s, to Kant's *Lectures on Ethics Collins*, we can see this new strategy in action, in the form of an argument for an early version of the categorical imperative that provides us with an overview of the strategy in *Groundwork I* and *Groundwork II*. Kant takes it for granted that we to some extent know the moral law and accept its authority. The task is instead one of clarifying the *source* of the moral law — and specifically whether morality is grounded in sensibility or understanding — and of clarifying what the *nature* of this moral law is. Kant thus asserts that "morality rests either on empirical or intellectual grounds," before setting out to determine which of these it is, and he also asks "what, then, is the supreme principle of morality whereby we judge everything, and in what way does moral goodness differ from every other sort of goodness?" (V-Mo/Collins, AA 27: 252). He turns first to empirical grounds, to systematically reject all of them, telling us first that "If a system of ethics is based on empirical grounds, it rests either on inner or outer grounds, drawn from the objects of inner and outer sense" (V-Mo/Collins, AA 27: 253). The inner grounds are physical feeling, or self-love, and moral feeling, with Kant listing Epicurus among the proponents of the former and Shaftesbury and Hutcheson among the proponents of the latter. Kant rejects both of these inner empirical grounds because of their *contingency*: regarding the possibility of the moral law resting on self-love, Kant explains by way of *reductio* that if the imperative to not lie rested on self-love, then the imperative "would run: You are not to lie only if it brings harm your way, but if it profits you, then it is permitted"; likewise, if the imperative rested on moral feeling "then anyone not possessed of a moral feeling so fine as to produce in him an aversion to lying would be permitted to lie" (V-Mo/Collins, AA 27: 254). These are the inner grounds, which concern the sensible faculties of feeling and desire and on which Kant will focus in *Groundwork I* before he there turns to practical reason stripped of such sensible feelings and desires, i.e., before he turns to what is effectively *pure* practical reason. Kant next moves on, in the *Lectures on Ethics Collins*, to the *outer* empirical grounds, of education and government, with which he will begin *Groundwork II*. Here again, the contingency of the imperatives disqualifies them on intuitive grounds, with Kant again arguing by *reductio*: "were the prohibition of lying to rest upon education or government, then anyone educated or living under a regime where lying is permitted, would be at liberty to lie" (V-Mo/Collins, AA 27: 254). These "outer empirical grounds" concern the sensible faculty, in particular, of *cognition*, on which Kant focuses at the start of *Groundwork II* before turning to practical reason, at which point he will there reject *instrumental* practical reason because its hypothetical imperatives are, again, contingent and incompatible with our idea of a moral imperative. What we see in Kant's *Lectures on Ethics Collins*, then, is that a lot of work *precedes* the point where — in the later *Groundwork* — we might try to extract the FUL from pure practical reason. Here Kant takes it for granted that we all agree that there is a moral law, and that we all agree that the authority of a moral law should not hinge on arbitrary empirical factors such as whether our government, our system of education, our feelings of morality, or our feelings of self-love just so happen to endorse this moral law. This rejection of such inner and outer empirical grounds leaves our practical reason free of all such arbitrary and possibly distorting influences, which means that our practical reason is now guided by the concern — anticipating FUL's test of impartiality — to have "all acts of my choice concur with universal validity" (V-Mo/Collins, AA 27: 257).

This brings us to the *Groundwork*, Kant's criticisms of the rationalist perfectionist Wolff, and Kant's argument leading up to FUL. In the *Groundwork*, Kant once again criticizes the manner in which the rationalist perfectionists' account is *empty*, consistent with Guyer's interpretation, telling us, for example, that the rationalists' concept of perfection "is empty, indeterminate, and hence of no use for finding in the immeasurable field of possible reality the maximum sum suitable for us" (GMS, AA 04: 443). No doubt this example of a purely formal ethical code would benefit from the addition of some matter, and now Kant would be able to offer something other than the moral feeling of the *Inquiry*, namely, the matter of humanity presented by Kant in the FH. But our question is whether Kant's own FUL has a similar fate, of requiring the matter of humanity as a reason or motivation for FUL. And on this score we find that the *Groundwork* once again points to the way in which the problem of the emptiness of rationalist perfectionism could be addressed, instead, by recourse to the distinction in kind between understanding and sensibility — without relying on the matter of humanity. Turning to the Preface to the *Groundwork*, we find Kant there arguing that the rationalist perfectionists have failed precisely because they have not properly cordoned off a priori reason from merely empirical motives. In other words, Kant here criticizes the rationalist perfectionists *not* for having *too little content*, as he of course also does elsewhere, but once again for having *too much empirical content*. In other words, he is criticizing the rationalists for being *bad rationalists*, i.e., for *not being rationalist enough*, allowing empirical content to mix in indiscriminately under the heading of "indistinct" understanding for lack of a distinction in kind between understanding and sensibility:

> they do not distinguish the motives which, as such, are presented completely a priori by reason alone and are properly moral from the empirical motives which the understanding raises to general concepts merely by the comparison of experiences. Rather, they consider motives irrespective of any difference in their source; and inasmuch as they regard all motives as being homogeneous, they consider nothing but their relative strength or weakness. In this way they frame their concept of obligation, which is certainly not moral, but is all that can be expected from a philosophy which never decides regarding the origin of all possible practical concepts whether they are a priori or merely a posteriori. (GMS, AA 04: 391)

Kant also draws an analogy to general logic versus transcendental logic, telling us that

> Wolff has not taken into consideration any special kind of will, such as one determined solely by a priori principles without any empirical motives and which could be called a pure will, but has considered volition in general [...]. And thereby does his propaedeutic differ from a metaphysics of morals in the same way that general logic, which expounds the acts and rules of thinking in general, differs from a transcendental philosophy, which treats merely of the particular acts and rules of pure thinking, i.e., of that thinking whereby objects are cognized completely a priori" (GMS, AA 04: 390).

A look at Kant's *Critique of Pure Reason* helps us to appreciate Kant's point here. There Kant tells us that

> [...] a distinction between pure and empirical thinking of objects could also well be found. In this case there would be a logic in *which one did not abstract from all content of cognition*; for that logic that contained merely the rules of the pure thinking of an object would exclude all those cognitions that were of *empirical content* [...] while general logic, on the contrary [...] deals only with the form of the understanding" (KrV, A 55/B 79–A 56/B 80).

Kant's point is that general logic does not consider the *pure thinking of objects* (to the exclusion of empirical thinking of objects), as does *transcendental* logic, but instead sticks to rules for thinking in general; and that, by parallel, rationalist perfectionism *does not consider the pure, properly moral contributions of reason* (again, to the exclusion of empirical incentives), as does Kant's moral philosophy, but instead sticks to "volitions in general." While transcendental logic, Kant's a priori ethics, general logic, and perfectionistic rationalism, are therefore all *formal* in one sense, of being stripped of all *empirical* content, transcendental logic and Kant's a priori ethics *offer pure (but not empirical) content*, providing new insight into how reason thinks a priori about objects and volition.

Turning to FUL, we find that Kant approaches this formulation of the categorical imperatives from two starting points. In *Groundwork I* Kant famously starts from what he takes to be the universally shared conviction that a good will, or action from duty in our case (as finite rational beings), has special, unconditioned, and unqualified value. This is a *self-evident* starting point for Kant, not a conclusion reached by argumentation, placed boldly in the first sentence of the *Groundwork*, and it has pulled in readers for over two hundred years rather than alienating them. Kant never wastes a moment with talk of a skeptic about the value of a good will, and, indeed, when discussing examples of a heroic good will, he often describes the way in which we one and all take inspiration from the hero in question and wish to be more like them — even if not in their dangerous predicament. We readily recognize the unconditional value of the good will and are presumably interested to learn more about the *nature* of the moral law that directs such a will, *not whether there is a moral law at all.* Once Kant has taken us through the remainder of his usual Elimination of Sensibility Procedure, systematically (and not haphazardly) touring the various sub-faculties of the faculty of sensibility and rejecting self-love and moral feeling as possible sources of determination of such an unconditionally valuable good will — just as he had done in his *Lectures on Ethics Collins* when he toured our inner empirical grounds, rejecting self-love and moral feeling as inner empirical grounds — he has now effected the elimination of that part of our sensibility that might guide practical reason in a merely *instrumental* manner, so that he has now "deprived the will of every impulse that might arise for it from obeying any particular law" (GMS, AA 04: 402). It is at this point, after all of this argumentation, that Kant presents the Formula of Universal Law (FUL) for the first time, asserting that "there is nothing left to serve the will as principle except the universal conformity of its action to law as such, i.e., I should never act except in such a way that I can also will that my maxim should become a universal law" (GMS, AA 04: 402).

We now return to the beginning: Guyer's point about the relationship between the FUL and FH. In Guyer's words,

> Kant has also seemed to many to advocate an insistence upon obedience to law for its own sake, an insistence upon blind obedience to law that in the twentieth century just ended has been associated with the destruction of everything for which the Enlightenment stood. A profound paradox can be avoided only if it can be shown that Kant intended obedience to universal law to be mandatory solely as a necessary condition for the realization of human freedom (KFLH, 1).

What we have now seen, in addition to Guyer's strong evidence for his interpretation, is another, partly overlapping possibility. Kant's early engagement with the rationalist perfectionists revealed Kant's desire to add substance to the rationalist perfectionists' formal account, as Guyer notes, but it also revealed Kant's determination to draw a sharp line where none existed in the perfectionists' account between pragmatic imperatives and moral imperative — moral imperatives of a *categorical* sort. With the introduction of his distinction-in-kind between sensibility and understanding around 1769, Kant could now systematically identify all sensibly-grounded imperatives per se as inadequate to the categorical demands of morality. And so when Kant discusses the moral law directly (as in *Groundwork II*) or the good will as determined by the moral law (as in *Groundwork I*), he can now confidently and safely guide us from each of these starting points, with an awareness always of the unique, unconditioned nature of the moral, through a systematic process of elimination of those faculties of sensibility whose products have in Kant's view adulterated all previous ethics. Guiding us from the self-evident starting point of the unconditioned value of a good will (or the unconditioned demands of the moral law) past these empirical shoals, Kant brings us to the high ground of pure practical reason, of practical reason now operating *without* the leading — or misleading — strings of empirical desires that compromise our impartiality. Kant chooses to couch this resulting impartiality in terms of universality, and certainly his at-times tortured account of "contradictions in conception" — and just as importantly the uncritical reception of it on the part of some of Kant's interpreters — invites questions about blind rule worship or blind deference to Kant, but what he describes is (as ought to be the case, given that Kant adamantly insists that he never dreamed of inventing a new moral law, but only to render the moral law clearer (KpV, 8n)) a new and arguably improved version (in its inclusion of duties to self and both negative and positive duties to all) of familiar, well-worn, and well-respected, if unclear and incomplete, moral concepts of impartiality and fairness as found in the following: the Golden Rule, Hume's Judicious Spectator, and Rawls's Original Position, among many others. We could move to justify the FUL as a necessary means to FH and the value of humanity, but recall that the value of humanity is at least arguably attributable to humanity's capacity for a good will, whose goodness would then, again, be presupposed within FH. So now the advantage of one strategy is to render FUL a means to respecting and promoting humanity (as something capable of a good will), and that of the other to render FUL a form of willing that itself constitutes a good will. Either way, the unconditioned value of the good will is self-evident and universalizable willing is our moral path forward, and on that harmonious note I will end this essay, on the happy occasion of honoring both Immanuel Kant and Paul Guyer.

References

Guyer, Paul (2000). *Kant on Freedom, Law, and Happiness*, Cambridge.
Wuerth, Julian (2014). *Kant on Mind, Action, and Ethics*, Oxford.
Wuerth, Julian (2021). "Categorical Imperative." In *The Cambridge Kant Lexicon*, ed. by Julian Wuerth, Cambridge, 67–94.

Kate Moran
A Modest Defense of the Personal Highest Good

Abstract: In this essay, I argue that Kant has a philosophically coherent notion of the highest good for the individual, where this is understood as an object of practical reason, but not as an object of moral action. Crucially, only an object of moral action demands a causal relationship between virtue and happiness, according to which the former brings about the latter. The account I argue for here requires only a conditioning relationship between virtue and happiness. As such, the account I offer is a relatively scaled-back version of the highest good for the individual. Nevertheless, I think it can serve as the basis for a kind of practical belief.

Keywords: highest good, happiness, postulates, laws of nature

The main argument I want to make in this paper is that Kant has a philosophically coherent notion of the highest good for the individual, where this is understood as an object of practical reason, but not as an object of moral action. The highest good for the individual consists of an individual agent's maximal virtue, combined with as much happiness as is consistent with such virtue for that agent. As such, it is the object of practical reason for individual rational yet sensible agents whose reason necessarily seeks a kind of totality. This notion of the highest good is distinct from an account of the highest good according to which moral action brings about happiness generally, within a moral community and over the course of history. A crucial distinction between the two accounts, I will argue, is that only the second account demands a causal relationship between virtue and happiness, according to which the former brings about the latter. The first account only requires a conditioning relationship between virtue and happiness, according to which the former limits the how much of the latter an agent can enjoy.

It would be more accurate to say that these are the various relations between virtue and happiness that Kant should have recognized in each account of the highest good. Infamously, Kant insists on a causal relationship between the individual agent's virtue and her happiness in the Dialectic of the *Critique of Practical Reason*. This assertion, for which he gives only the suggestion of an argument, is at the foundation of much of what is confusing and problematic about the argument for the postulates of pure practical reason in that text. First and foremost, it is what leads some philosophers to wonder if Kant is slipping into heteronomy, since it introduces the prospect of an agent's own happiness into her deliberations about moral action.[1] Beyond this, it is at the basis of Kant's arguments for the existence of God and the immorality of the soul, which, if not exactly 'train wrecks', are something like an overly-exuberant stumbling.[2] Nevertheless, there are passages in which Kant does not obviously insist on a causal relationship between individual virtue and individual happiness, and in these passages, he offers his most philosophically coherent notion of the individual highest good.

The discussion that follows proceeds in three sections. In the first, I review some of the problems that commentators, including Paul Guyer, have noted about Kant's individualist account of the highest good. I also give an overview of the account of the highest good that places its realization in the moral community, and discuss some of its interpretative virtues. Despite the strengths of the latter account, I suggest that there are independent reasons to take seriously the notion of the highest good for the individual. In the second section, I make a case for a personal account of the highest good that does not insist on a causal connection between virtue and happiness. In the final section, I explore what agents might have practical grounds to believe on the basis of this individualist account of the highest good.

A virtue, I hope, of the account I offer here is that it allows two distinct notions of the highest good to exist side by side, since each is concerned with a different set of questions. One is a set of questions about the totality of virtue and happiness for a rational and sensible agent. The other is a set of questions about whether and how we can expect virtue to bring about happiness. Kant's exuberant mistake in the *Critique of Practical Reason* is to attempt to allow the first account of the highest good to answer the questions belonging to the second.

---

[1] Most notably, perhaps, Lewis White Beck: "Kant simply cannot have it both ways. He cannot say that the highest good is a motive for the pure will, and then say it is so under the human limitation that man must have an object which is not exclusively moral (for there is nothing moral in happiness except insofar as its condition is worthiness to be happy, and even then the moral value lies in the worthiness, not the enjoyment)." (Beck: *A Commentary on Kant's Critique of Practical Reason*, Chicago 1960, 244.) But the concern is probably overblown, since whatever happiness is part of the agent's highest good *qua* individual is still conditioned by morality. In Kantian terms, the maxim of self-love is still subordinate to the morality (RGV, AA 06: 36.21–23).

[2] Cf. Paul Guyer's discussion of the third section of the *Groundwork*: "Naturalistic and Transcendental Moments in Kant's Moral Philosophy," *Inquiry* 50, 2007, 444–464, 445.

1 Two Accounts of the Highest Good

In the Dialectic of the *Critique of Practical Reason*, Kant famously characterizes the highest good as the complete good for rational and sensible agents,[3] and as the object of practical reason.[4] Importantly, the highest good is, for Kant, composed of two parts: first, perfect or maximal virtue, and second, the greatest degree of happiness that is consistent with such virtue. On this point, Kant sets himself apart from the ancients, who attempted to fuse the two into a relation of identity. For the purposes of the discussion in this essay, it is important to take note of Kant's objection to the Stoic account of the relationship between virtue and happiness. As Kant interprets that view, "consciousness of one's virtue is happiness."[5] Kant agrees with his picture of the Stoics that consciousness of one's virtue — to the extent that this is at all possible — generates a positive feeling, something that he characterizes as 'contentment'.[6] But this is not the same as happiness. Without entering into the robust debate about how best to understand the Kantian conception of happiness, we can minimally note that Kantian happiness includes the satisfaction of various needs and desires that originate from human beings' sensible nature.[7] Kant's notion of the highest good thus brings together the perfection of our rational nature (virtue) with as much satisfaction of our sensible nature (happiness) as is consistent with such virtue.

The preceding is only a rough sketch of Kant's general conception of the highest good, and the details of this conception do not always remain stable or consistent throughout the texts in which he grapples with it. In particular, Kant sometimes argues that the highest good must find its realization within the individual agent, i.e. that the highest good describes the perfect virtue of an individual, and the greatest degree of happiness that is consistent with such virtue for that individual. This is what Guyer sometimes describes as the 'composite' account of the highest good, since on such an account "the highest good [is] the compound object of a compound being, the natural pursuit of personal happiness restricted by the moral requirements to fulfill duty and achieve virtue as the condition for worthiness to be happy."[8] In the Dialectic of the *Critique of Practical Reason* this composite account

---

[3] KpV, AA 05: 111.01.
[4] KpV, AA 05: 109.20.
[5] KpV, AA 05: 111.24–25.
[6] KpV, AA 05: 117.28–29.
[7] For a discussion of these, see Timmermann, Jens: *Kant's Will at the Crossroads*. Oxford 2022, chapter 2.
[8] Guyer, Paul: "Ends of Reason and Ends of Nature." In *Kant's System of Nature and Freedom*. Oxford 2005, 169–197, 183.

of the highest good is meant to give us practical grounds for belief in several items of special metaphysics. Kant's argument for this conclusion is that the highest good, as the object of practical reason, is morally necessary. In particular, Kant argues, virtue and happiness together exist together in a synthetic relationship in which virtue brings about happiness. As he describes it, the connection between virtue and happiness "is found in virtue's producing happiness as something different from the consciousness of virtue, as a cause produces an effect."[9] Of course, this causal connection between virtue and happiness is not one that we typically see in this world, so Kant thinks we must postulate God as the author of laws of nature that conjoin virtue and happiness in a causal relation, and we must postulate the immortality of the soul, since perfect virtue — the first part of the highest good — is impossible in this life.

There are too many problems with this argumentative strategy to give an exhaustive account of them here. It makes good sense to point out that, as sensible agents, we aim at our own happiness, and that this happiness is in fact good insofar as an agent is worthy of it, i.e. insofar as that happiness is consistent with morality. But it is not at all clear what argument there is for the claim that morality demands a reward of happiness, or that an individual's virtue must bring about that individual's happiness, either in this life or the next. This is a point I will return to in more detail in the next section.

Setting that point aside for the moment, there is a further question about why Kant should insist that we are incapable of complete virtue at any moment of our existence. The most straightforward way of interpreting this claim is that we are constitutionally incapable of perfect virtue, owing to the fact that we are in the rather unfortunate position of having to drag our sensible selves around with us everywhere we go, which in turn means that we are constantly beset by temptation in the form of inclination. This would be to equate virtue with holiness, which Kant seems happy to do in the *Critique of Practical Reason*,[10] but it is not how he describes virtue in other texts. In the "Doctrine of Virtue," for example, he describes virtue as a kind of moral strength in the face of contrary inclination, not as the expulsion of inclination.[11] And, as Guyer has argued in detail, this account of moral progress or reform is not consistent with Kant's later account in the *Religion Within the Limits of Mere Reason*, where he argues instead that we are capable of a change of heart

---

9 KpV, AA 05: 111.16–17.
10 KpV, AA 05: 122.09.
11 TL, AA 06: 405.15–16.

in this life, though we cannot be certain of this fact since the change of heart occurs noumenally.[12]

On a similar note, if Kant's assumption is that our sensible nature is all — or even most — of what stands in the way of achieving perfect virtue, it is not clear why he needs to posit an eternal afterlife in order for agents to achieve perfect virtue. One might have thought that the task would be accomplished once one has had a few moments of respite from one's sensible self. We might wonder, in other words, what there is left for an agent to do once she is rid of inclination. But then we face a new problem from the other side of the highest good: once an agent is rid of sensibility and inclination, it is not clear how she can achieve happiness, at least as far as we understand it. Recall that Kant argues that we must postulate God as the author of laws of nature that guarantee the connection between virtue and happiness. But whatever happiness agents might enjoy once they've gotten rid of sensibility, it would not seem to be the sort of happiness brought about or conditioned by laws of nature.[13]

Finally, even if we ignore these problems, the argument seems to aim too high, doxastically speaking. Why assume that moral agency requires a guarantee of this object, such that practical belief in the existence of God and the immortality of the soul is warranted? Why, in other words, wouldn't something like practical belief in the mere possibility of the highest good and its postulates be sufficient?

These sorts of worries have led several commentators, including Paul Guyer, to argue for an interpretation according to which the highest good is best understood as a collective end, achievable over the course of human history. The highest good does not, in other words, describe a state of hoped-for existence for an individual, but rather the state of affairs brought about by the shared moral striving of the moral community. As such, Guyer sometimes calls this a 'unitary' account of the highest good, where happiness is "the condition that results from the successful pursuit of our ends, the promotion of happiness, not our personal happiness alone but the happiness of all insofar as that is compatible with the freedom of each."[14] Setting aside Kant's arguments regarding the postulates of pure practical reason in the Dialectic of the second *Critique*, there is ample textual evidence for such an

---

12 Guyer, Paul: "Kant, Mendelssohn, and Immortality." In Thomas Höwing (ed.), *The Highest Good in Kant's Philosophy*. Berlin/Boston 2016, 157–179, 171.
13 Cf. Guyer, Paul: "Kantian Communities." In *Virtues of Freedom: Selected Essays on Kant*. Oxford 2016, 276–302, 285.
14 Guyer, "Ends of Reason," 184.

interpretation of the highest good. In the *Critique of Pure Reason*, Kant likens the highest good to a 'moral world' in which morality is 'self-rewarding,' for example.[15]

Interpretatively, there is much to be said for this approach. First, it makes sense of the causal relationship that Kant suggests with regard to the relationship between virtue and happiness. For example, in the "Canon" of the first *Critique*, Kant acknowledges that "reason has causality with regard to freedom in general but not with regard to the whole of nature"[16] and identifies the highest good as "the world as it would be if it were in conformity with all moral laws (as it can be in accordance with the freedom of rational beings and should be in accordance with the necessary laws of morality) a moral world."[17] The 'world as it would be if it were in conformity will all moral laws' would be one in which agents observe perfect duty and perform imperfect duties, including imperfect duties to others. Since imperfect duties to others are duties to adopt the ends of others as one's own, and since accomplishing one's ends brings about — or perhaps just is — happiness, on Kant's understanding, there is a relatively straightforward connection between the two components of the highest good. Of course, this is not to say that any individual who is virtuous will also be happy, nor is it to suggest that moral action will be able to overcome natural misfortune. Still, the moral world described would be one in which happiness generally follows from virtue. Second, for reasons closely related to those above, this interpretation makes sense of Kant's claim that belief in at least one of the postulates of pure practical reason is a 'need of reason'.[18] If we have an obligation to do our part to bring about the highest good, then this would seem to place some demands on practical reason from an agential standpoint. Minimally, it would seem that some belief in the possibility of the highest good is required, along with whatever postulates necessary to secure this belief. While belief in the immortality of the soul is not required on this account, practical belief in laws of nature that link virtue and happiness is arguably warranted.[19] Finally, it is arguably a virtue of this interpretation that it makes the highest good a human project, and a project around which human institutions — both formal and less formal — can be organized. Not least of all, this includes the possibility that the organization of civil society can contribute to humanity's progress toward the highest good.[20]

---

[15] Guyer, "Ends of Reason," 184, and "Kantian Communities," 283.
[16] KrV, A 807/B 835.
[17] KrV, A 808/B 836.
[18] KpV, AA 05: 142–143.
[19] For this reason, Guyer is reluctant to call even the interpretation of the highest good that places its fulfillment in this world a 'secular' notion of the highest good. See "Kantian Communities," 284.
[20] Guyer: "Kantian Communities," 300.

As encouraging as all of this may be from the standpoint of a moral agent hoping that her moral strivings may eventually come to something and successfully produce happiness, it is likely to be cold comfort to us when we consider any individual virtuous life in isolation — including our own. To put the point in intentionally broad terms for now, there does seem to be something wrong or deficient about a virtuous life that is not also happy. Colloquially, at least, the point is made in terms of justice: it seems unjust or unfair that a virtuous life should not also be happy.

Of course, there a straightforward response open to the Kantian, namely to remind the agent concerned with 'justice' that the moral law doesn't aim at happiness. A major lesson of Kantian ethics, they might say, is that some degree — perhaps even a great degree — of personal sacrifice is demanded by the moral law. To insist that there is something unjust about a virtuous life that is not happy is just to allow sensibility to elbow its way in to our deliberations. It is essentially a psychological impulse, perhaps — to appropriate Bernard Williams' turn of phrase — we might even characterize it as a kind of 'squeamishness' about the demands of morality.[21]

There is an obvious sense in which all of this is true. But it is crucial to observe that much of what the Kantian might find objectionable about this demand for 'justice' is that there should be a causal link between virtue and happiness — either in the form of virtue naturally bringing about happiness (i.e., through laws of nature), or in the form of some divine reward for virtue. But if we set that assumption aside for a moment, I think there is still room for a set of important observations about the relation between virtue and happiness in the individual. In particular, since virtue and happiness are both ends of a rational yet sensible agent, there is a straightforward sense in which a life that is virtuous and happy is better than a life that is virtuous and unhappy. Seen from the standpoint of impartial reason the latter comes closer to a totality sought by practical reason. Thus, while the prospect of one's own happiness alone cannot serve as the object of moral action, the Kantian conception of practical reason will still judge there to be something lacking whenever a virtuous individual is not also happy to the degree that is consistent with that virtue. In what follows, I will attempt to unpack this point and try to discover what, if anything, follows from it.

---

21 See Williams, Bernard: "A Critique of Utilitarianism." In Smart, JJC: *Utilitarianism: For and Against.* Cambridge 1973, 77–151, 102.

2 Virtue, Happiness, and the Individual

Kant is not a Stoic: happiness matters to Kant, in the sense that it is a good in its own right — at least insofar as happiness is consistent with morality. Moreover, we should not, I think, presume that Kant's rejection of Stoicism is a reluctant concession to our sensible nature. To be sure, there are passages in which Kant seems to regret sensibility — for example, his claim in the *Groundwork* that the inclinations "are so far from having an absolute worth ... that to be entirely free from them must ... be the universal wish of every rational being",[22] or even the suggestion in the "Dialectic" discussed above, that our sensible nature makes virtue impossible at any moment of our existence. Guyer rightly observes that, seen in light of passages like these, the notion of the "composite" highest good within the individual "makes it sound as if virtue is our sole object as rational beings, but happiness our object of desire as finite beings, for which virtue must, somehow yet somewhat grudgingly, make room."[23] But I don't think that this is the view that Kant should take, nor do I think it is the view he always takes. In the *Religion*, for example, Kant claims that "Considered in themselves natural inclinations are good, i.e. not reprehensible".[24] And consider the following well-known passage from the "Dialectic" of the *Critique of Practical Reason*:

> [Virtue] is not yet, on that account, the whole and complete good as the object of the faculty of desire of rational finite beings; for this, happiness is also required, and that not merely in the partial eyes of a person who makes himself an end but even in the judgment of an impartial reason, which regards a person in the world generally as an end in itself. For, to need happiness, to be also worthy of it, and yet not to participate in it cannot be consistent with the perfect volition of a rational being that would at the same time have all power, even if we think of such a being only for the sake of the experiment.[25]

To my mind, this is one of Kant's better arguments concerning the 'composite' or individual highest good. He is wise to consider the matter third-personally, even, as he says, from "the standpoint of an impartial reason." This removes any danger that the concern for happiness is a heteronomous one. The point I take the passage to be making is fairly straightforward: given Kant's commitments in his practical philosophy — that we are end-setting creatures with the capacity to limit or constrain our pursuit of our particular ends according to the demands of pure practical

---

22 GMS, AA 04: 428.14–16.
23 Guyer: "Ends of Reason," 184.
24 RGV, AA 06: 58.01.
25 KpV, AA 05: 110.22–31.

reason — there are two very different things that constitute what is good for us. The first of these is virtue, and the second of these is happiness. Of course, the former is a necessary end, so it will always condition the latter. That is just to say that not all happiness is good; only happiness that is consistent with morality is good. But it is still good. From the standpoint of an impartial practical reason, a life that is maximally virtuous yet unhappy is thus less good — in the sense that it participates in less overall goodness — than a life that is maximally virtuous and also happy. Again, this is not to say that we ought always to seek own own happiness when we act, or even that we need some guarantee of eventual happiness in order to act morally. Both of those claims, I think, would be heteronomous. Nevertheless, we do recognize a kind of deficiency when a virtuous life is not also happy. Much of what makes this passage a good argument, on my view, is the modesty of its claims. In particular, there is no claim — yet — that happiness must follow from virtue, or even that agents should be rewarded for their virtue. Kant's arguments start to go off the rails once he begins to substitute these sorts of claims for the more modest observation that there is a deficiency in evidence when a virtuous person does not also "participate" in happiness. The best way, I think, to interpret the composite highest good, then, is not as a grudging concession to sensibility, but as something more like an embrace of it — insofar as it can be kept within the constraints of morality, of course.

So far, then, the point is merely that there is a coherent notion of the highest good for the individual, namely, the state of being maximally virtuous and simultaneously being as happy as such virtue allows. But it is also important to be clear about what this notion of the individual highest good does not include. First, there is no claim that this state of affairs exists or will exist. As we are all too well aware, it is a state that few — if any — achieve or enjoy, and Kant is under no delusions about this fact.[26] Second, it does not include a claim that there is much that any of us can do to bring about the highest good for ourselves or other individuals, aside from simply striving for virtue. In particular, there is no claim that it is our business to attempt to distribute happiness according to individuals' virtue, since we cannot know other people's motives in order to discern their virtue. And, in any case, Kant thinks that if doling out happiness according to virtue is anyone's job, it must be

---

26 Kant's most memorable acknowledgment of this fact is perhaps the discussion of the Spinozist in the *Critique of the Power of Judgment*: "Deceit, violence, and envy will always surround him, even though he is himself honest, peaceable, and benevolent; and the righteous ones besides himself that he will encounter will, in spite of all their worthiness to be happy, nevertheless be subject by nature, which pays no attention to that, to all the evils of poverty, illnesses, and untimely death, just like all the other animals on earth, and will always remain thus until one wide grave engulfs them all together..." (KU, AA 05: 452.20–27).

God's.[27] Third, despite what Kant will sometimes say, there is no philosophical reason to presume that there exists a causal relationship between individual virtue and happiness. If a person were to achieve the individual, composite highest good in the sense described so far, it would be to some degree because other agents are acting virtuously, but, presumably, it would also be largely a matter of luck. Nor is there any reason to think that virtue will cause or bring about happiness indirectly, via divine justice. Again, this is something that Kant will sometimes suggest, but it is not part of this basic notion of the individual highest good, according to which the best state of existence for creatures like us is one in which maximal happiness is conditioned by maximal virtue.

These observations bring us to a crucial distinction that, I think, Kant only sometimes takes heed of — much to the detriment of his arguments in the Dialectic, in particular. This is a distinction between object of practical reason and object of moral action. The object of practical reason refers merely to the totality sought by practical reason that we have been discussing thus far, and it is what Kant refers to when he says, for example, that "pure practical reason ... seeks the unconditioned for the practically conditioned."[28] The object of moral action is what we can or should expect to result from virtuous action — whether this is understood in terms of a 'unitary' highest good, accomplished within the moral community, or whether it is understood in terms of divine reward for virtue.

Kant sometimes argues about the highest good as if the object of practical reason and the object of moral action were one and the same, but they are not. Kant's mistake, in other words, is to move too quickly from the wholly correct thought that virtue necessarily stands in a conditioning relationship with happiness to the further claim that virtue necessarily stands in a causal relationship with happiness. Of course, there is a perfectly legitimate reason to make this argumentative move when it comes to the virtue and happiness of the moral community, since agents acting virtuously will be treating others as ends in themselves and promoting the ends of others via the imperfect duty of beneficence. This will have a general causal tendency to promote the happiness of the moral community, taken as a whole.[29] But there is no similar or corresponding reason to assume a causal connection between virtue and happiness when it comes to the individual highest good. There, the relation is one of conditioning, not causation. Nevertheless, Kant clearly thinks that the relationship is causal in the "Dialectic":

---

27 *E.g.* V-Mo/Collins, AA 27: 450.30–35.
28 KpV, AA 05: 108.07–08.
29 Cf. "Ends of Reason," 184–185.

> Two determinations necessarily combined in one concept must be connected as ground and consequent, and so connected that this unity is considered either as analytic (logical connection) or as synthetic (real connection), the former in accordance with the law of identity, the latter in accordance with the law of causality. The connection of virtue with happiness can therefore be understood in one of two ways: either the endeavor to be virtuous and the rational pursuit of happiness are not two different actions but quite identical, in which case no maxim need be made the ground of the former other than that which serves for the latter; or else that connection is found in virtue's producing happiness as something different from the consciousness of virtue, as a cause produces an effect.[30]

In this passage, Kant seems only to consider two possibilities: either virtue and happiness are related to one another through a relation of identity, in which case their unity is analytic; or they have have a 'real' connection, in which case their unity is synthetic. As we have already seen, Kant rejects the ancients' way of proceeding, i.e. to assume a relation of identity, and insists instead on a 'real,' synthetic relation. But now Kant also insists that any synthetic connection between virtue and happiness must be causal. What is Kant's argument for this causal claim? Certainly, we can imagine two properties being related to one another without insisting on a causal relation between them: a mug might be blue and ceramic, but one property doesn't bring about the other. Presumably, Kant's claim in the passage above relies on the fact that we are not here considering two theoretical entities or properties, but rather two ends of practical reason. And since practical reason concerns itself with action — or causally bringing about certain effects in the world — any practical relation must be causal. As Kant explains,

> Now, this combination is (like every other) either analytic or synthetic. Since, as has already been shown, the given combination cannot be analytic, it must be thought synthetically and, indeed, as the connection of cause and effect, because it concerns a practical good, that is, one that is possible through action.[31]

The claim makes a certain amount of sense. When we think of the way that two actions are related to one another, we often think of the relation of means and ends. If my practical end is mastering the backstroke, then various other actions will be 'related' to this as means — for example, getting in the pool, and moving my legs and arms in a particular way. On the face of things, then, there is a case to be made for suggesting that non-identical actions relate to one another in a causal way. But we might add that my ends and actions can be related in other ways, too. If I want to master the backstroke, but I also want to meet a deadline for a separate project,

---

30 KpV, AA 05: 111.06–18, my emphases.
31 KpV, AA 05: 113.19–22, my emphasis.

then the things I need to do in order to master the backstroke may have to be put on hold until I finish the project. My end of finishing the project might, in other words, limit or condition my end of mastering the backstroke, at least temporarily. Or, to bring the point closer to the case at hand: I may need to put my end of mastering the backstroke on hold in order to fulfill a moral obligation — for example to rescue someone in distress.

Kant's insistence that virtue and happiness must be related to one another causally is, of course, a key premise in his argument for the postulate of the existence of God. Because virtue and happiness must relate to one another in this way, Kant argues that we must posit God as the author of laws of nature that secure this causal connection. But, as I have been suggesting, there is no need to insist on the causal premise. Notably, Kant does not always seem obviously to insist upon it himself. In his discussion of the highest good in the Canon of the Critique of Pure Reason, Kant sketches the relation as follows:

> Leibniz called the world, insofar as in it one attends only to rational beings and their interconnection in accordance with moral laws under the rule of the highest good, the realm of grace, and distinguished it from the realm of nature, where, to be sure, rational beings stand under moral laws but cannot expect any success for their conduct except in accordance with the course of nature in our sensible world. Thus to regard ourselves as in the realm of grace, where every happiness awaits us as long as we do not ourselves limit our share of it through the unworthiness to be happy, is a practically necessary idea of reason.[32]

Kant's description of the 'realm of grace' in this passage does not seem to suggest a strong causal connection between virtue and happiness. Rather, he describes it as a realm 'where every happiness awaits us' [wo alle Glückseligkeit auf uns wartet] as long as we do not make ourselves unworthy of happiness. To be sure, the notion of happiness 'awaiting' us is potentially ambiguous: it could 'await us' qua reward for virtue, in which case Kant would be suggesting a kind of causal relation between virtue and happiness. More plausible, to my mind, is an interpretation according to which the 'realm of grace' is simply a maximally happy place, in which agents are free to enjoy happiness, so long as they are worthy of it. On that interpretation, there is no causal connection between virtue and happiness. The source, as it were, of happiness is not related to a person's virtue, either naturally or through divine reward. Nevertheless, a person's virtue will condition that happiness, i.e. make her deserving of it.

---

[32] KrV, A 812/B 840.

The passage from the *Critique of Pure Reason* is not an outlier. Kant reportedly says something very similar in the second set of *Mrongovius lectures*, given around the time of the publication of the *Groundwork*:

> The mistake [of the ancients] in this was that they tried to squeeze the two parts into one, when in fact they are entirely different; for the one indicates the worth of the person, whereas the other indicates the worth of the condition. The two are heterogeneous and both have therefore their own particular sources. But there must be a link; otherwise they can never be together. Now, this link is religion. The ancients tried to do without religion, but it did not work. Only through religion may I hope that someone who makes himself worthy of happiness can actually be happy.[33]

In this passage, as in the previous passage, there does not appear to be any mention of a causal connection between virtue and happiness. Of course, since the source of the passage is a set of transcribed lecture notes, it is important not to put too much weight on particular words that Kant did or did not say. Still, the general sense of the passage is interesting for its similarity with the discussion of the ancients in the Dialectic, and for the way that it appears to diverge from that discussion. As in the "Dialectic," Kant observes that the ancients made the mistake of identifying virtue with happiness — trying to squeeze two parts into one. Notably, however, Kant also observes that virtue and happiness have two different sources, a claim that is, to be sure, consistent with a causal claim, but perhaps friendlier to a more moderate claim that virtue and happiness are two very different ends, each with its own source. Despite the fact that virtue and happiness have two different sources, Kant insists that there 'must be a link' between them, offering what sounds like a tautology for an argument: if there is no link, then they can never be together. Again, we don't know if this is what Kant actually said, but a charitable way of interpreting Kant's claim would be to point to the totality that practical reason seeks, a totality in which virtue and happiness are found together. Since virtue and happiness have distinct sources — at least as far as the individual is concerned — Kant thinks we need to look to religion for some hope of an association between the two. Why or whether we need such hope is its own question, which I consider in the next section.

When it comes to the hoped-for relation between virtue and happiness, I suspect that the argumentative and interpretative waters are muddied somewhat by the fact that Kant does consistently observe that there is no reason to think that there exists a causal connection between virtue and happiness for the individual agent in this world. The passage from §87 of the *Critique of the Power of Judgment*

---

33 V-Mo/Mron II, AA 29: 600 (translated Jens Timmermann and Stefano Bacin).

quoted in the footnote above is certainly an example, as is the following observation in the *Critique of Pure Reason*:

> But since the obligation from the moral law remains valid for each particular use of freedom even if others do not conduct themselves in accord with this law, how their consequences will be related to happiness is determined neither by the nature of things in the world, nor by the causality of actions themselves and their relation to morality; and the necessary connection of the hope of being happy with the unremitting effort to make oneself worthy of happiness that has been adduced cannot be cognized through reason if it is grounded merely in nature, but may be hoped for only if it is at the same time grounded on a highest reason, which commands in accordance with moral laws, as at the same time the cause of nature.[34]

Still, to observe correctly that there is no causal connection to be found between two ends with distinct sources is not to say that these must be somehow connected causally. There is a difference between two sorts of arguments, and I suspect they often bleed into one another in Kant's writing and our interpretation of him. The first kind of argument begins with the premise that individual virtue and happiness must be causally connected and then observes that such a causal connection does not appear to hold in the order of nature. The second kind of argument merely observes that virtue and happiness are both goods — virtue, of course, being necessarily good, and happiness only conditionally good — and observes, with some regret, that there is no predictable, causal, way to bring the latter about by pursuing the necessary end of morality. Indeed, pursuing the end of virtue will often have just the opposite result when it comes to the pursuit of happiness. The first type of argument makes the accomplishment of happiness a project for an afterlife; the second makes the accomplishment of happiness a matter of luck.

There are, in other words, two distinct possible interpretations of Kant's claim in the *Religion* that "it cannot be a matter of indifference to reason how to answer the question, What is then the result of this right conduct of ours?"[35] On the first interpretation, the question whose answer cannot possibly be a matter of indifference is about the causal outcome of our moral actions. Of course, there is an obvious Kantian sense in which agents should be indifferent to the answer to this question, so long as it is about the happiness we can expect to enjoy individually as a result of our moral actions. The causal interpretation of the question makes sense, in other words, when we understand it to be a question about the happiness we can expect to produce in the moral community as a result of our moral actions. But there is another way of understanding the question whose answer 'cannot be a

---

34 KrV, A 810/B 838.
35 RGV, AA 06: 05.03–04.

matter of indifference', and this is a question about whether we can, as individuals, ever reasonably hope to be happy and virtuous simultaneously — whatever the source of that happiness. This, in other words, is a question about how close to the complete good of practical reason any individual can hope to come.

Of course, it is less than obvious what follows from the preceding observations about the object of practical reason when it comes to what we can reasonably conclude or hope for when it comes to metaphysical questions concerning the existence of God or the immortality of the soul. Because the relationship between personal virtue and happiness is conditioning, and not causal, there does not seem to be any separate duty to bring about the personal highest good, and so the conclusions involving the "need of reason" mentioned earlier do not follow. Still, there may be a need of reason specific to the personal highest good, understood as a totality of practical reason where virtue conditions happiness. We turn to that question next.

3 The Need of Reason

Closely related to the preceding questions about how, precisely, to understand Kant's notion of the highest good is another set of questions about what Kant's account of the highest good gives us license to believe, or at least hope, on practical grounds. As Kant explains in the *Critique of Practical Reason*,

> [A] need of pure practical reason is based on a duty, that of making something (the highest good) the object of my will so as to promote it with all my powers; and thus I must suppose its possibility and so too the conditions for this, namely God, freedom, and immortality, because I cannot prove these by my speculative reason, although I can also not refute them.[36]

Speculative reason, as Kant takes himself to have shown decisively in the *Critique of Pure Reason*, cannot make claims about the existence — or non-existence — of God, freedom, and the immortality of the soul. However, Kant now argues, his arguments regarding morality and the highest good give us practical grounds for belief in them. Indeed, Kant has already argued in the Preface to the *Critique of Practical Reason* that we have practical knowledge of freedom, since this follows immediately from our awareness of morality's bindingness.[37] Now Kant argues that practical belief in God and the immortality of the soul can be supported by the needs of pure practical reason.

---

36 KpV, 05: 142.19–24.
37 KpV, AA 05: 04.07–10.

This 'need of reason' argument, as Kant presents it, clearly relies on the assumption that virtue and happiness are related to one another causally. The version of the highest good described in this passage is both the object of my will and something that ought to be promoted with all of my powers. As Kant explains in his response to Thomas Wizenmann, it is precisely because we have a duty to bring about the highest good that this object of our will is not a mere wish, but rather a need of reason.[38] Duty tells us that we have an obligation to promote the highest good, so it must be possible. Hence, we are licensed to have a practical belief in those things that make it possible — in particular, the immortality of the soul and the existence of God. There are many questions that we can raise about the argument — for example about the various modalities of belief that Kant mentions: Is belief in God as the author of laws of nature required to support the possibility of the highest good, or might something like belief in the mere possibility of such an author be sufficient? However we come down on questions like these, it is still the case that the argument only works if our understanding of the highest good is that of an object of moral action, not just an object of practical reason. To put a finer point on things, if we understand the highest good in terms of a totality that practical reason necessarily aims at, it seems like it will be much closer to the kind of hope or wish that Wizenmann accuses Kant of placing at the foundation of his argument. Practical reason must, necessarily, aim at virtue, and it does, definitionally, aim at happiness. But if we think of these as causally disconnected, then any duty to bring about the highest good cannot go beyond the duty that we already knew we had, namely, to be as virtuous as possible.

This is why I tend to think that the need of reason passage works better — but not perfectly — with the 'unitary' or immanent conception of the highest good. On that account, we can understand it as our duty to bring about both components of the highest good, i.e. we can understand the highest good as the object of moral action. Of course, the argumentative payoff of this interpretation is less impressive, since there is no need to posit the immortality of the soul if progress can happen over the course of many generations. But my sense is that it is enough to support a practical belief that there is a general causal connection between virtuous action and happiness. On one level, such a causal connection is not very mysterious: we aim at bringing about happiness when we adopt the ends of others as our own, for example. Still, I think, there is room for a kind of faith that our actions will be effective, i.e. that the causal relation between adopting and acting for the sake of another's ends and their happiness will generally exist.

---

38 KpV, AA 05: 143n.

However, as I have been arguing, Kant is not really at liberty to say that the connection between virtue and happiness in the individual is a causal connection. He is right to say that it is an object of practical reason in a certain sense. Specifically, it describes the complete good for an individual, and thus constitutes a coherent object for practical reason, which is bound to seek this kind of totality. But there isn't really any sense in which we should think that virtue causes happiness in the individual, so any metaphysical conclusions about what must be the case in order to make possible that causal connection are blocked. Now, we might think that this leaves us with a rather underwhelming conclusion regarding the individual, 'composite' highest good. Yes, perhaps there is a sense in which it is a coherent goal for practical reason to strive toward, but if this is really all there is to it, there isn't much we can conclude from this observation. Nevertheless, I think there are Kantian reasons to be suspicious of a universe that is wholly indifferent to the highest good, understood individually. Perhaps a somewhat lighthearted example may help illustrate this thought.

Imagine two teams engaged in a competitive game. Two aims will guide the conduct of each team. First, each team must follow the rules of the game. But there is a rather obvious sense in which the teams are not there simply to follow the rules of the game; they are also trying to win the game. These two aims model the aims of practical reason. The first — following the rules of the game — is necessary and conditions the other. A team that scores more points by cheating hasn't won, or at least this is how an 'impartial reason' will judge the matter. But, again, the teams are each there to win, so we can say that the complete good for each team is to play according to the rules of the game and win the game. Though the necessary end of playing by the rules conditions the end of winning the game, it does not bring it about that a team will win the game. Nor should we expect it to, since there is no necessary causal link between playing by the rules and winning the game: these are separate aims. Nor is it the case that either team needs a guarantee of winning in order to play the game. Indeed, in a game that doesn't allow a tie, each team knows that one team will not win. Still, I think there is a fairly fundamental sense in which it would not make sense for a team to play the game at all if there were reason to suspect that they could never win. Suppose a referee has been bribed always to rule against their team, for example. 'What's the point of playing,' they might say, 'if we don't stand a chance of winning?' Of course, one hears such things when teams are in a slump or down on their luck, but that is probably hyperbole: in those cases, there is still a chance of winning, even if it is distant and would require a good deal of effort or luck.[39] The case I have in mind is a case in which a team has knowledge — sufficient objective grounds for assent — that they cannot win, despite their best efforts, and despite their playing by the rules.[40] I think it would be close to impossible, if not simply nonsensical, to play the game under these conditions.

I suggest the 'need of reason' as it relates to the individual highest good is like this. Just as there is no reason to think that following the rules of a game will bring about a team's victory, there is no reason to expect that happiness will follow from virtue — either via natural causal laws, or through divine reward. Still, practical reason tells us that there is a complete good for creatures like us, and we necessarily act in a way that seeks this complete good. Thus, from the standpoint of a practical reason that seeks this totality, it would be a serious problem if we knew that the complete good were impossible. It would be impossible, if not nonsensical, to act if we knew that the world were wholly inhospitable to the pursuit of the individual highest good, understood as this totality. To be clear, this is miles away from the claim that we could only act if our own happiness were assured. But it would be more than just discouraging if we lived in a world whose laws were set up in such a way that virtue could not be coupled with happiness, even if only fortuitously. This, at a minimum, is what I take Kant to be saying in the *Mrongovius lectures* when he says there must be a link between virtue and happiness.

In those lectures, Kant says that it is the role of religion to ensure this link between virtue and happiness. In light of this discussion of the need of reason, it is not wholly obvious what this might mean. If it means that we have to hope that virtuous individuals will achieve happiness in an afterlife, then this may not be altogether satisfying, since, as we have already noted, it is not clear how happiness can be part of a non-sensible afterlife. Perhaps Kant means that it is the role of religion to give us some rational belief that the world is at least hospitable to the virtuous agent's happiness, i.e. that when it comes to the laws of nature, things are set up so that virtue and happiness can coexist. Again, if we think of the highest good in the individual as a kind of totality as opposed to a causal relationship between virtue and happiness, then the stakes are somewhat lower. We do not have to have rational belief in laws of nature that ensure a causal connection between virtue and happiness in the individual. We just need a belief in laws of nature that don't get in the way of these two things coexisting. This is not a minor point: it is precisely

---

39 Alternately, in such cases, we might make sense of the team forging ahead despite the impossibility of winning if we say that they are playing for the sake of their teammates, or the love of the game, *etc.*
40 Chignell, Andrew: "Belief in Kant." In *Philosophical Review* 116 (3), 2007, 323–360.

because Kant's moral system decouples virtue and happiness when it comes to the ground of moral obligation that there is some need to seek this reassurance from the perspective of practical reason, considered as a whole.

To go beyond what Kant says on the matter, I think it is possible to extend the observation to human institutions. As we have already noted, it is clearly not our business to reward individuals for their virtue, or to try to make sure that virtuous people are happy and vicious people are unhappy. Nevertheless, seen from the standpoint of the needs of reason associated with the individual highest good, it would be practically undermining to devise institutions that make the world inhospitable to the happiness of virtuous agents — think back to the corrupt referee, for example.

4 Conclusion

It bears emphasizing that I do not take myself to be doing strict exegesis in this discussion: that is, I do not think that the arguments I've presented are able to 'make sense' of everything that Kant says about the highest good, and untangle and confusions or apparent problems with his arguments. For example, Kant clearly thinks that there is a causal connection between individual virtue and individual happiness in the Dialectic of the *Critique of Practical Reason*, and I think there is no reason for him to help himself to this premise. There is also a clear sense in which the account of the individual highest good I have been offering here works less well alongside Kant's claims that we have a duty to pursue the highest good,[41] or — relatedly — the claim that the object of the highest good can be understood already as part of the ground of moral action.[42] It is clear to me that the systematic, this-worldly interpretation of the highest good does a much better job of making sense of these claims. My main goal in this paper is simply to argue that we should not allow the obvious strengths of the systematic account to let us discard an individualist account altogether. There are good Kantian reasons for maintaining a pared-down, individualist notion of the highest good — understood as a totality of practical reason that every rational and sensible agent wants to participate in. At a minimum, this account of the highest good can give us a sense of what a good life looks like for a Kantian agent. Beyond this, it may provide Kantian grounds for belief in laws of nature that are at least not hostile to the fortuitous coupling of virtue and happiness, and it may give us good reason not to devise institutions that are hostile to happiness.

---

41 KpV, AA 05: 126.01.
42 KpV, AA 05: 109–110.

References

Beck, Lewis White (1960). *A Commentary on Kant's Critique of Practical Reason*, Chicago.
Chignell, Andrew (2007). "Belief in Kant." *Philosophical Review* 116 (3), 323–360.
Guyer, Paul (2005). "Ends of Reason and Ends of Nature." In *Kant's System of Nature and Freedom*, Oxford, 169–197.
Guyer, Paul (2007). "Naturalistic and Transcendental Moments in Kant's Moral Philosophy." *Inquiry* 50, 444–464.
Guyer, Paul (2016a). "Kant, Mendelssohn, and Immortality." In *The Highest Good in Kant's Philosophy*, ed. by Thomas Höwing, Berlin/Boston, 157–179.
Guyer, Paul (2016b). "Kantian Communities." In *Virtues of Freedom: Selected Essays on Kant*, Oxford, 276–302.
Timmermann, Jens (2022). *Kant's Will at the Crossroads*, Cambridge.
Williams, Bernard (1973). "A Critique of Utilitarianism." In *Utilitarianism: For and Against*, ed. by J.J.C. Smart, Cambridge, 77–151.

Wiebke Deimling
The Passion for Freedom and the Passion for the Ultimate Means

Abstract: Paul Guyer takes the freedom to set ends to be the fundamental value in Kant's moral philosophy. He also argues that we have a passion for freedom that can ground the "content and the possibility of morality". This paper raises and addresses questions for the idea that a passion can serve as a ground of a Kantian account of morality. It argues that we can best answer these questions if we take into account both Kant's passion for freedom and its complements: the passions for honor, power, and possession, which Kant presents as desires to use others as the ultimate means. I suggest that the passions spur reflection, engage reason, and lead to moral development. Kant's picture has similarities both to Hume's account of the calm passions and to Rousseau's account of moral development facilitated by the generally harmful amour-propre.

Keywords: passion, inclination, freedom, fundamental value, naturalized

1 Introduction

Paul Guyer argues that the freedom to set ends is the fundamental value in Kant's moral philosophy. He also raises worries about the a priori grounding of Kant's ethics and expresses hope that it can be naturalized. In chapter twelve of *Virtues of Freedom* Guyer makes a suggestion for what a key piece of such a naturalization might look like. He argues that a "passion for freedom" can ground the "content and the possibility of morality"[1] in Kant's account.

Commentators have objected both to the claim that freedom is the fundamental value in Kant's account and to the idea of naturalizing Kant's ethics. My main goal here is not to determine what grounds morality on Kant's account — whether it is freedom or reason. And it is not to conclusively answer whether naturalizing Kant's ethics is possible and/or desirable. Instead, I am interested in the details of such a naturalization. Specifically, I want to look at the potential role a passion for freedom might play. In chapter twelve of *Virtues of Freedom* Guyer acknowledges that a passion, as Kant describes it, cannot ground morality as it is. It has to be modified.[2]

---

1 Guyer, Paul (2016), *Virtues of Freedom*, 202.
2 Guyer (2016), 207.

Here I raise and address challenges posed by what Kant says about the passion for freedom and the passions in general.

a) How can a passion for freedom ground the "content and the possibility of morality" if Kant dismisses the passions as morally corrosive?
b) Kant introduces external freedom, the freedom *from* interference by others, as the main object of the passion for freedom. But it is the freedom to set ends that Paul Guyer introduces as the fundamental value in Kant's moral philosophy. How then does the passion for freedom relate to this fundamental value?
c) If a passion for freedom needs to be refined or modified — with the help of reason — to ground moral action, what motivates such a refinement? Can we account for this motivation within a naturalized version of Kant's moral philosophy?

I argue that we can best address these questions if we foreground Kant's claim that the passions are social, i.e. they are directed at other human beings as their objects.[3] The passion for freedom is a desire to be free from the interference of others in setting our ends.[4] Complementary to this Kant introduces passions *to* interfere in the lives of others, i.e. desires to use their recognition, labor, and resources to satisfy our own desires: "Ehrsucht," "Herrschsucht," "Habsucht".[5] Kant stresses that the passions are the most powerful of our desires. The reason for their strength, according to Kant, is that human beings are the ultimate means to our ends and the ultimate threat to our freedom. Their recognition, labor, and resources are so valuable to the achievement of our ends that they are not comparable to other means. And their interference in our lives is an incomparably greater threat to setting and pursuing our own ends than any other threat we might encounter. Kant's passion for freedom is tied to the recognition that we are the ultimate means for other human beings. And, conversely, to the recognition that other human beings are the ultimate means for us. I suggest that the experience of the tension between the passion for freedom and the passion to use others as the ultimate means can provide a first step in grounding morality within a naturalized Kantian account. I argue that Kant's understanding of the passion for freedom has similarities both to Hume's account of the calm passions, as Guyer suggests, and to Rousseau's account of amour-propre.

In what follows section 1 briefly sketches Guyer's views on the value of freedom and the role of the passion for freedom in Kant's account. It also outlines two

---

[3] Anth, AA 07: 268.
[4] Ibid.
[5] Anth, AA 07: 273f.

criticisms of Guyer's view. Section 2 spells out questions a) through c) raised above. Section 3 lays out Kant's theory of the passions as social and suggests answer to questions a) through c). And section 4 notes some challenges for naturalizing Kant's moral philosophy.

2 Paul Guyer on Freedom and the Passion for Freedom

In the introduction to *Kant on Freedom, Law and Happiness* Guyer gives this description of his project in the book: "my primary concern in almost all of what follows is to document and to understand Kant's commitment to the normative thesis that freedom is our fundamental value".[6] This description could also serve to characterize Guyer's work on Kant's practical philosophy as a whole. The most explicit statement of this commitment in Kant's own corpus can be found in the student notes on Kant's lectures on ethics: freedom is "der innere Wert der Welt."[7] His scholarship explains how the fundamental value of freedom fits into the overall picture of Kant's moral philosophy and traces how Kant develops his mature view on the value of freedom. Guyer contrasts his own emphasis on freedom in his reading of Kant with an emphasis on reason. He points to the following passage from the *Naturrecht Feyerabend* where Kant himself contrasts freedom and reason. "Wenn nur vernünftige Wesen können Zweck an sich selbst seyn; so können sie es nicht darum seyn, weil sie Vernunft, sondern weil sie Freiheit haben. Die Vernunft ist bloß ein Mittel."[8] He characterizes Kant's moral philosophy as a kind of perfectionism according to which we should strive to maximize freedom — our own as well as that of others. We are to perfect "our own will or power of choice"[9] and aim for "the maximization of intra- and interpersonal freedom".[10]

Guyer is famously pessimistic about Kant's arguing for and building upon transcendental idealism. And for Kant's moral philosophy in particular, Guyer takes Kant's efforts to provide an a priori grounding for the moral law to be largely

---

6 Guyer, Paul (2000), Kant on Freedom, Law and Happiness, 7.
7 V-Mo/Mron, AA 27: 1482; cited by Guyer in *Kant on Freedom, Law and Happiness*, 96 and in *Virtues of Freedom*, 130. Guyer cites this passage often, Frederick Rauscher counts eight different places (see Rauscher, Frederick (2018), "Moral Realism and the Inner Value of the World," 154).
8 V-Mo/Mron, AA 27: 1321.
9 Guyer (2016), 79.
10 Guyer (2016), 87.

unsuccessful.[11] But on the flip side, Guyer sketches how a core of Kant's ethics might stand untethered from Kant's doctrine of transcendental idealism. And he suggests that Kant's own work, especially Kant's account of freedom in his early work[12] and his attention to "the empirical etiology of moral action" in the *Metaphysics of Morals* and the *Anthropology*,[13] can give us guidance for this untethering.

In thinking through the details of Kant's "empirical etiology of moral action" in *Virtues of Freedom* Guyer arrives at a surprising conclusion: Hume's and Kant's accounts of moral motivation turn out to be similar: "Kant [...] shares with Hume the idea that morality is founded upon a passion for freedom and that reason is not an end in itself but rather a means to the gratification or at least the refinement of that passion."[14] Guyer suggests that in a naturalized version of Kant's moral philosophy we can ground morality in this desire for freedom while acknowledging an important role for reason in shaping and directing this passion. He makes clear that he prefers this naturalized account: "I personally find Kant's theory that we have a nominally free will that always allows us to do the right thing no matter what our inclinations a fairy-tale. But I find his empirical theory that we come to be able to act morally only by refining and cultivating our native inclination towards our own freedom entirely plausible."[15]

As I noted above, scholars have criticized both Guyer's emphasis on freedom and his interest in naturalizing Kant's ethics. Heiner Klemme, for example, argues that "freedom qua value cannot function as a premise on which Kant's ethics are based; [f]or all the importance of freedom, Kant's ethics revolve around reason".[16] According to Klemme, it is only through reason that we can have the idea of freedom and it is only by taking an interest in reason that we can take an interest in freedom.[17] He further claims that "recasting Kant's ethics in naturalism cannot do justice to two ethical intuitions central to Kant's moral philosophy: [t]he notion of one's own will and the idea that even the worst human being deserves our moral respect".[18] And Fred Rauscher argues that freedom cannot be the "inner value" of the world if this commits Kant to moral realism. For Kant, according to Rauscher, "there is no property of objects 'absolutely valuable' that is independent of either

---

11 See e.g. ibid., 164f.
12 Guyer, Paul (2007), "Naturalistic and Transcendental Moments in Kant's Moral Philosophy."
13 Guyer (2016), 207.
14 Guyer (2016), 208.
15 Guyer (2016), 215.
16 Klemme, Heiner F. (2024), "Maximizing Freedom? Paul Guyer on the Value of Freedom and Reason in Kant," 59.
17 Klemme (2024), 65f.
18 Klemme (2024), 59.

the transcendental moral agent or the empirical moral agent".[19] Further, so Rauscher, it is unclear how we would become aware of such a property, which would have to be accessible either through inner or outer intuition.[20]

3 Kant on the Passions and the Passion for Freedom

In his published *Anthropology* as well as in the student notes we have on Kant's anthropology lectures, Kant does indeed introduce a passion for freedom. He characterizes it as original to us: infants are born with it.

> Ja das Kind, welches sich nur eben dem mütterlichen Schooße entwunden hat, scheint zum Unterschiede von allen andern Thieren blos deswegen mit lautem Geschrei in die Welt zu treten: weil es sein Unvermögen, sich seiner Gliedmaßen zu bedienen, für Zwang ansieht und so einen Anspruch auf Freiheit (wovon kein anderes Thier eine Vorstellung hat) sofort ankündigt.[21]

Kant says that infants already have a "dunkle[] Idee" of freedom or a representation analogous to it.[22] Humans in all societies have a passion for freedom in different forms and to different degrees.[23] If we take Guyer's suggestion that freedom is the fundamental value for Kant, we can take Kant to suggest that we have an original desire for this fundamental value. This idea of an original passion for freedom fits well with the emphasis Kant puts on freedom in his characterization of the human species in the "Anthropologische Charakteristik".[24] More clearly than in the published *Anthropology* we find the connection between freedom and the character of the human species in the later student notes we have on Kant's lectures. What sets the human species apart from animals is human freedom: "der Mensch ist von Natur frei und alle Menschen sind sich von Natur aus *gleich* — Hierinn weicht der Mensch auch von der tierischen Natur ab"[25]. But Kant's general discussion of the passions might leave us hesitant to ground the "content and

---

19 Rauscher (2018), 166.
20 Rauscher (2018), 160.
21 Anth, AA 07: 268.
22 Ibid.
23 Ibid.
24 Anth, AA 07: 330.
25 V-Anth/Mron, AA 25: 1419.

the possibility of morality"[26] in this original tendency. Let me return to the questions raised in the introduction.

a) One of the main messages (if not *the* main message) that Kant conveys is that passions are morally corrosive. They are particularly strong kinds of desires that do the most damage to freedom,[27] they are "Krebsschäden für die reine praktische Vernunft", and "ohne Ausnahme böse".[28] Passions, on Kant's account, are especially harmful desires for two reasons. (1) They give us tunnel vision. Kant defines a passion as follows. "Die Neigung, durch welche die Vernunft verhindert wird, sie in Ansehung einer gewissen Wahl mit der Summe aller Neigungen zu vergleichen, ist die Leidenschaft (passio animi)."[29] (2) They are long lasting because they are compatible with "der ruhigsten Überlegung".[30] Only human beings are capable of passion because they presuppose a maxim.[31] They do not merely blind with their intensity as a bout of excitement or anger might. But they drive us to one-sidedly restructure how we think about our choices to accommodate pursuing the passion. Other passions, that Kant presents alongside the passion for freedom, are morally suspect at best: "Rachbegierde," "Ehrsucht," "Herrschsucht," and "Habsucht."[32] What Kant says about the passion for freedom in particular is unflattering as well. He says that for the natural human being, before the forming of a civil society, the passion for freedom is "die heftigste" among all passions. It leads to a "Zustand des beständigen Krieges in der Absicht andere so weit wie möglich von sich entfernt zu halten".[33]

b) Kant describes the object of the passion for freedom as our own external freedom. As the passage with the infant cited above shows, this includes freedom from physical restriction. But it also means making choices informed by one's own notion of happiness as opposed to another person's. "Wer nur nach eines Anderen Wahl glücklich sein kann (dieser mag nun so wohlwollend sein, als man immer will), fühlt sich mit Recht unglücklich."[34] According to Guyer the freedom at the core of Kant's moral philosophy is the freedom to set ends — our own and that of others.[35] But the freedom to set ends, and the inclusion of others' freedom, are

---

26 Guyer (2016), 202.
27 Anth, AA 07: 265 ("der Freiheit den größten Abbruch thun").
28 Anth, AA 07: 266f.
29 Anth, AA 07: 265.
30 Ibid.
31 Anth, AA 07: 266.
32 Anth, AA 07: 268f.
33 Ibid.
34 Anth, AA 07: 268f.
35 Guyer (2016), vii.

largely absent from Kant's discussion of our passion for freedom in both the published *Anthropology* and the student notes.

Passions are of course not the only desires Kant discusses in his anthropology. So what about a desire for freedom that is *not* a passion in the sense just discussed? In his published *Anthropology* Kant never discusses such a desire. But in the student notes on Kant's anthropology lectures we do find a "formal inclination" to freedom, which is introduced before the treatment of the passions. It is introduced along with the formal inclination to "capacity", which is the desire to have the means to satisfy our inclinations.[36] Kant explains the formal inclinations as follows.

> Alle unsere Neigungen können in formelle und materielle eingetheilt werden. Die formellen gehen ohne Unterschied der Gegenstände auf die *Bedingungen*, unter denen wir überhaupt unsere Neigungen befriedigen können; sie haben also keinen besonderen Gegenstand; die materiellen sind die welche in Ansehung des Gegenstandes bestimmt sind.[37]

Unfortunately, the discussion of the formal inclinations is brief and fails to give us a good sense of the role Kant takes them to play. And the discussion of the formal inclination to freedom, like that of the passion for freedom, is at a first glance focused only on external freedom as opposed to the freedom to set ends. The formal inclination to freedom desires the "Entfernung alles Widerstandes, nach seiner eigenen Neigung zu handeln".[38] Kant says that it is a "formale negative Neigung".[39] I will return to these formal inclinations in the next section.

c) Guyer acknowledges that Kant's characterization of the passions conflicts with understanding the passion for freedom as fundamental to moral action. He suggests that a passion for freedom providing a foundation for morality cannot be a passion in Kant's sense of the term "passion." It has to be modified. It is "a passion that must be expanded from our own freedom to the freedom of all and which, so expanded, can no longer be called a passion but needs another name."[40]

But this modification is not trivial. Guyer says that reason guides us in refining the passion: the passion for freedom "gradually becomes governed by reason".[41] We might ask about the motivation for this modification. What drives us to refine

---

36 "capacity" is "Vermögen", V-Anth/Mensch, AA 25: 1141, V-Anth/Mron, AA 25: 1354, and V-Anth/Busolt, AA 25: 1520.
37 V-Anth/Mensch, AA 25: 1141, "capacity" is "Vermögen"; see also V-Anth/Mron, AA 25: 1354, and V-Anth/Busolt, AA 25: 1520.
38 V-Anth/Mensch, AA 25: 1141; see also V-Anth/Mron, AA 25: 1354.
39 Ibid. and V-Anth/Busolt, AA 25: 1520.
40 Guyer (2016), 207.
41 Guyer (2016), 215.

or expand our passion for freedom in this way? Would the answer to this question depend on Kant's transcendental idealism and/or his attempt to give morality an a priori grounding? In other words, one might worry that we have failed to find a path to naturalizing Kant's ethics after all. Guyer distinguishes between the content and the form of morality: "freedom is the material good, but since the formal principle of morality is universality, it is the freedom of all, not just oneself, that is the object of morality."[42] But this leaves open some questions. How do we ground "the formal principle of morality" in a naturalized Kantian account? What motivates us to universalize? Are we naturalizing just Kant's account of moral motivation or all of Kant's ethics?

4 The Passions as Social Desires

I have already discussed how passions on Kant's account are particularly strong kinds of desires that are morally problematic because they give us tunnel vision and are long-lasting. But there is another defining characteristic that Kant ascribes to the passions: they are social. The passions are "nur von Menschen auf Menschen gerichtete Neigungen […], so fern diese auf mit einander zusammenstimmende oder einander widerstreitende Zwecke gerichtet […] sind".[43] And indeed the examples Kant gives are of desires that have other human beings as their object either directly or indirectly. I will discuss the passions for freedom, honor, power, and possession ("Freiheitsneigung als Leidenschaft", "Ehrsucht," "Herrsucht," "Habsucht").[44] As I have shown above, Kant describes the passion for freedom as the desire to be free from others' interference. The passions for honor, power, and possession are desires *to* interfere in the life of others. He describes them as "Neigung[en] zum Vermögen, Einfluß überhaupt auf andere Menschen zu haben"[45] and explains the particular desires as follows.

> Ehrsucht ist die Schwäche der Menschen, wegen der man auf sie durch ihre Meinung, Herrschsucht durch ihre Furcht und Habsucht durch ihr eigenes Interesse Einfluß haben

---

42 Guyer (2016), 209.
43 Anth, AA 07: 270.
44 Anth, AA 07: 268f.; in the published *Anthropology* Kant also adds the passion for sex, for revenge, and the passion to socially engage in games or hobbies ("Neigung des Wahnes als Leidenschaft") and in the lecture notes we find a few other examples as well: e.g. being in love ("verliebt" seen as opposed to "lieben") V-Anth/Mensch, AA 25: 1122 and sympathy ("Mitleid") V-Anth/Mensch, AA 25: 1132 as passions.
45 Anth, AA 07: 271.

kann. — Allerwärts ein Sklavensinn, durch den, wenn sich ein Anderer desselben bemächtigt, er das Vermögen hat, ihn durch seine eigenen Neigungen zu seinen Absichten zu gebrauchen.[46]

The claim that passions are always about human beings might strike us as odd and one might worry that Kant conflates humans being the only ones to *have* passions, which he also wants to claim,[47] with passions being only *about* human beings. This might be the reason why the social nature of the passions is rarely discussed in the scholarship.[48]

But if we think through Kant's discussion of the passions, it becomes clear that it is their fundamental characteristic. The social nature of the passions explains the other characteristics Kant ascribes to them. Passions are strong and long-lasting 1) because what other human beings can give us is so much more valuable to setting and pursuing our own ends that other conditions and resources are not even comparable and 2) because control by others is a much greater threat to setting and pursing our own ends than any other threat. We can see this line of thought expressed in the student notes on Kant's lectures.

> Alle Leidenschaften gehen auf Menschen, und niemals auf Sachen. Wir haben wohl Neigungen zu Sachen, z.B. zu starken Getränken, zur Faulheit etc.; aber alle diese werden nicht Leidenschaften, denn die wahren Leidenschaften beziehen sich auf Menschen, weil diese die allergrößten Mittel zur Befriedigung unserer Neigungen sind. Vereinigte Bemühung der Menschen kann unsere Neigungen befriedigen oder verhindern, mehr, als irgend etwas [...]. Die Natur enthält nicht so wohl Stoff zur Befriedigung unserer Neigungen, als vielmehr die *Erfindungskraft* der Menschen.[49]

Others are the ultimate means ("die allergrößten Mittel") to us and we are always in danger of becoming the ultimate means for others. It is striking how much Kant's discussion of the passions foreshadows later discussions of oppression and exploitation. He gives the following description of the passion for power and the passion for possession.

> Der Einfluß der Gewalt beruht auf der Furcht anderer [...]. Geld ist ein Mittel, andere durch ihren Eigennutz in meine Absicht zu ziehen, so, daß jeder Mensch all seine Bedürfniße

---

46 Anth, AA 07: 272.
47 Anth, AA 07: 266.
48 Though there are some exceptions of scholars who do pick up on the social dimension of Kant's discussion. See Borges, Maria (2021), "Passions and Evil in Kant's Philosophy" *as well as* Wood, Allen (2009), "Kant's Fourth Proposition: the unsociable sociability of human nature."
49 V-Anth/Mensch, AA 25: 1142.

> durch Geld befriedigen kan. Daher ist Geld ein Mittel zu allen den Zwecken zu gelangen, die durch die vereinigten Bemühungen der Menschen möglich sind.[50]

The passion for freedom and the passions to use others as the ultimate means are tied to one another. We have a strong desire to be free from others' interference because we are the ultimate means for them, which gives them a strong motivation to exercise influence over us. On the flip side, the motivation of others to avoid our influence spurs our desire to exercise control. Further our particular desires and the ends they suggest are tied to the passion for freedom and the passions to use others as the ultimate means. When we desire to strike up a friendship we might be hesitant to share information because it could be used to the other's advantage and to our own disadvantage. And we might be tempted to misuse the information our friend shares as well (see Kant's own treatment of friendship in the *Metaphysics of Morals*[51]). Or when we desire to build a house, we might seek to avoid becoming the object of someone's greed — e.g. by avoiding an overcharging contractor. But we might also be tempted to ask our neighbors to provide unpaid labor in the building process and hence to make them a means to our end.

This tension between the passions helps us provide an answer to question c) above. We can explain what motivates us to modify our passion for freedom and to expand it to include as its object not just our own but also the freedom of others. The passions are bound to frustrate us: others are drawn to curtail our passion for freedom and they are drawn to resist our desire to make them the ultimate means to our ends. But this frustration spurs reflection. We start to think about the relationship between our own desires and those of others. Where do our ends conflict with the ends of others? Where do they coincide? What makes our ends valuable? What makes the ends of others valuable? And our reflection might take us further yet. We might conclude that pursuing ends as a community can take us much further than pursuing them only as individuals. This means that reason becomes engaged. Kant claims that reason "gradually develops" as our natural tendencies become governed by reason without being extinguished.[52]

When we reflect on our passions, we come to realize that we can only set and pursue our ends by managing the tension between our passions. We need to modify

---

50 V-Anth/Mensch, AA 25: 1146f.
51 MS, AA 06: 472.
52 V-Anth/Mensch, AA 25: 1123f. quoted in *Virtues of Freedom*, 214. Kant's example here is anger as an affect, which governed by reason continues to be useful for "self-preservation" but no longer has harmful effect for ourselves and others. I will come back to this idea in section 4.

and expand them. Because reason is a faculty of principles[53] we are led to universalize. We are led to desire the freedom to set ends in general — our own and that of others — as opposed to freedom from others' interference. And we are led to desire the general means to the realization of everyone's ends as opposed to others as the ultimate means to realize our own ends. In other words, the modified passions are desires for the freedom to set and pursue ends. And this is of course the kind of freedom that Guyer takes to be the fundamental value for Kant. The modified passions are no longer blinding and inflexible: we are able to weigh and balance our own ends and those of others and to moderate our desires and actions. And this means it is no longer a passion in the sense discussed above.

If we think of the passion for freedom as tied to the passions to use others as the ultimate means we can also respond to b) above. The object of the passion for freedom is freedom from the interference of others. But, more importantly, in his theory of the passions as a whole Kant is concerned with more than external freedom. The passions for honor, power, and possession concern our capacity *to* pursue our ends. And if we accept the account I have just given of our response to the passions, it drives us to desire freedom in general.

Finally in response to a) we can see that the passion for freedom can ground the "content and the possibility of morality" not just despite being morally corrosive but *because* it is morally corrosive. On the account I have given, the most fundamental desire for moral motivation is not the modified and expanded desire for freedom. Instead it is the original passion for freedom accompanied by the passions to use others as the ultimate means. What makes them morally problematic, the tensions they give rise to, also gives us motivation to reflect and to modify them.

I have given a description of what our passions might look like after we have reflected on them and modified them. But I should also say a few words about where in Kant's taxonomy of desires they belong. Specifically, I want to address the relationship between our passions — original and modified — and the formal inclinations I briefly discussed in the previous section. To point us back to what Kant says in the passage cited above, the formal inclinations are desires for "freedom" and "capacity" as the general conditions under which we can satisfy our desires.[54] We can now easily see how they turn into passions: the formal inclination for freedom (to live in accordance with our own, as opposed to others', desires) becomes a passion for freedom because others' interference is such a threat to choosing our ends freely; and the formal inclination to capacity (to have the means to satisfy our inclinations) becomes a passion to use others as the ultimate

---

53 KrV, A 299/B 356.
54 V-Anth/Mensch, AA 25: 1141.

means in its particular expressions (the passions for honor, power, and possession). But when we refine a passion, should we think of it as reverting to the same state it was before it became a passion? That is, are the modified passions for freedom and for using others as the ultimate means the same as the formal inclinations to "freedom" and "capacity"? What might speak in favor of this is that Kant is full of praise for the formal inclinations. Kant says that the formal inclination are the "ersten and vornehmsten Neigungen unter allen"[55] and that the passion for freedom is aimed at "das Höchste formale Gute des Natürlichen Zustandes"[56]. Nevertheless, I think we should resist the view that our passions once they are refined through reason are the same as the formal inclinations. First, it is not clear that formal inclinations are universal in the full sense that reason demands: their object seems to be only our own freedom and means to pursue ends. Second, what Kant might mean by the claim that these passions are "formal" is that they are implicit in our more particular desires. We are not independently aware of them. For example, we might be aware of our desire to pursue our own agenda at work as opposed to catering to our boss' preferences. But we are not aware of a general inclination to freedom before it becomes a passion, accompanied by a general tendency to shield and isolate us from others. In contrast to these implicit desires, we need to be aware of the modified passions for them to give rise to moral development. Ultimately though, according to Kant, the following is true. What we come to desire by reflecting on our passions and by modifying them under the guidance of reason is already present, even if implicitly and rudimentarily, in the pursuit of all of our desires: we desire to have the freedom to set and pursue ends.

I acknowledge that the picture I have just outlined is not explicit in Kant's writings on anthropology and moral philosophy. We have to read between the lines of these texts to see a positive role of the passions in moral motivation. He does, however, stress their role in cultural progress and moral progress when he develops his idea of unsocial sociability ("ungesellige Geselligkeit")[57] in his 1784 essay "Idea for a Universal History with a Cosmopolitan Aim". There he describes the human natural tendencies as follows.

> Er hat aber auch einen großen Hang sich zu vereinzelnen (isoliren): weil er in sich zugleich die ungesellige Eigenschaft antrifft, alles bloß nach seinem Sinne richten zu wollen, und daher allerwärts Widerstand erwartet, so wie er von sich selbst weiß, daß er seinerseits zum Widerstande gegen andere geneigt ist. Dieser Widerstand ist es nun, welcher alle Kräfte des Menschen erweckt, ihn dahin bringt seinen Hang zur Faulheit zu überwinden und, getrie-

---

55 Ibid.
56 V-Anth/Busolt, AA 25: 1520, cited by Guyer in *Virtues of Freedom*, 208.
57 IaG, AA 08: 20.

> ben durch Ehrsucht, Herrschsucht oder Habsucht, sich einen Rang unter seinen Mitgenossen zu verschaffen, die er nicht wohl leiden, von denen er aber auch nicht lassen kann. Da geschehen nun die ersten wahren Schritte aus der Rohigkeit zur Cultur [...]. Da [wird] der Anfang zur Gründung einer Denkungsart gemacht, welche die grobe Naturanlage zur sittlichen Unterscheidung mit der Zeit in bestimmte praktische Principien und so eine pathologisch-abgedrungene Zusammenstimmung zu einer Gesellschaft endlich in ein moralisches Ganze[s] verwandeln kann."[58]

The tension Kant describes here is familiar from what I have said above. Kant claims that our passions and the tension between them motivates action. But even more striking is Kant's claim that they begin to change our way of thinking ("Denkungsart") and eventually lead to practical principles. We have to approach the "Idea for a Universal History with a Cosmopolitan Aim" with caution. It is a popular essay, Kant takes it to presuppose teleological principles (nature as a whole has a purpose and the passions as our natural tendencies have the purpose of developing our species), and Kant does not take his account in the essay to be an accurate description of the actual unfolding of human history. But if we take what Kant says here together with what we do find in Kant's anthropology, Kant's own works do give us some guidance on how we might untether the foundations of Kant's moral theory from transcendental idealism.

As stated above, Guyer argues that Kant's view on what grounds morality is in fact similar to Hume's: a passion can ground the "content and possibility" of morality on both Hume's and Kant's view. I have agreed with Guyer, though I have suggested a more roundabout account of this grounding. But Kant's view also has substantial similarities with Rousseau's account of amour-propre. Both Rousseau's amour-propre and Kant's passions are morally corrosive, and they are harmful precisely *because* they are social in nature.[59] Allen Wood has stressed the similarity between Kant's account of the passions and Rousseau's account of amour-propre. He takes Kant to follow Rousseau in claiming that evil originates from our social condition.[60] But he rejects the idea that the passions and our unsocial sociability

---

58 IaG, AA 08: 21.
59 Though, while the passion to use others as the ultimate means is a product of culture, the passion for freedom, according to Kant, precedes culture, which also explains Kant's comment quoted above that the passion for freedom, before the forming of a civil society, brings about a "Zustand des beständigen Krieges in der Absicht andere so weit wie möglich von sich entfernt zu halten" AA 07: 268f. So technically, Kant's account has similarities to Hume's, Rousseau's, and Hobbes'. But Hobbes' account is lacking the account of moral development that I am highlighting in Rousseau's.
60 Wood (2009), 127f.

can ground morality or moral development which I have suggested here.[61] Wood says that on Kant's account of the passions are important to understanding what our particular obligations look like. It is important to realize that the "[moral] law turns out to be opposed to all the natural-social tendencies present in our unsocial sociability".[62] However, this does not mean that they provide grounding for morality. Morality, on Wood's reading of Kant, can only rely on a priori grounding. But at least on some readings of Rousseau amour-propre also spurs the development of our rational agency. Fred Neuhouser claims that "[a]mour-propre is a necessary, though not sufficient, condition of the formation of human beings in rational subjects". It motivates "the isolated beings of the state of nature to be drawn out of their solipsistic existence [...] and to act instead on principles that require them to take into account, and, so, to acknowledge the perspective of their fellow beings."[63] It is only because amour-propre helps us understand comparative value that we understand *equal* worth.[64] According to the reading I have provided here, on both Kant's and Rousseau's accounts it is our reflection on our harmful social desires and on the tensions they create that spurs moral development.

5 Problems with Naturalizing Kant's Account

The way I describe reflecting on the passions (reflecting on the consistency between ends, the value of ends, and setting ends in community with others) mirrors core tenets of Kant's canonical writings on moral philosophy. But the details of how we get from reflecting on our passions to moral principles and obligations are beyond the scope of this paper. I am not providing a naturalized version of Kant's moral philosophy but merely an account of what I take to be a key component — the passion for freedom and Kant's general account of the passions — and possible first steps. To make this clear I want to finish by noting three problems that need to be addressed if we are to succeed in the project of naturalizing from the starting point I have suggested.

Kant distinguishes between pragmatic and practical reasoning. The first involves hypothetical imperatives and the second categorical imperatives.[65] Categorical imperatives hold no matter what our inclination are, hypothetical imperatives

---

61 Wood (2009), 112.
62 Wood (2009), 120.
63 Neuhouser (2008), 218.
64 Neuhouser (2008), 223.
65 GMS, AA 04: 414.

are dependent on inclinations. I suggest here that a type of pragmatic reasoning — thinking about how we can fulfill our passions — can spur practical reason's activity. I think this is compatible with holding that they are two different kinds of reasoning. But I am not sure what Kant himself would say about it.

I have stated above that reason "gradually develops" as we reflect on our passions and the tensions between them. This picture of reason, as opposed to our fixed transcendentally ideal rational nature, of course fits well into the project of naturalizing Kant's account. In chapter twelve of *Virtues of Freedom* Guyer says the following "along with this passion [the passion for freedom], reason is also natural to human beings, and naturally develops as they mature".[66] And he quotes from the *Menschenkunde* lectures where Kant explains that our original desires gradually become governed by reason without becoming extinguished and while remaining useful to us. Kant claims there that the human being is "dazu berufen, daß sich nach und nach in him die Vernunft ausbilde".[67] But much work remains to be done to see if reason as a natural, gradually developing, faculty can stand independently from our transcendentally ideal rational nature and to work out how many of the characteristics Kant ascribes to reason can apply without transcendental idealism.

I have intended my account here to be both an account of moral motivation and an account of the grounding of morality. But one might argue that I have provided only the former. Kant makes much of the distinction between motive and incentive.[68] And in the "Doctrine of Virtue" in the *Metaphysics of Morals* he is careful to limit the role of moral feelings to incentives: they play a role in his account of moral motivation but the true motive is the moral law.[69] The role of the passions I have suggested is different from the role Kant ascribes to moral emotions in the "Doctrine of Virtue". The passions spur reflection, they lead us to involve reason and facilitate reason's development. But one can surely raise further questions about the relationship between the passions and reason I have outlined here.

---

66 Guyer (2016), 214.
67 V-Anth/Mensch, AA 25: 1123f.
68 GMS, AA 04: 427.
69 MS, AA 06: 399f.

6 Conclusion

This paper discussed Paul Guyer's suggestion that the passion for freedom Kant introduces in his anthropology can ground the "content and the possibility of morality"[70] in Kant's account. I take Guyer to understand this suggestion as a key step to naturalizing Kant's account. Kant's discussion of the passion for freedom within the context of his theory of the passions raises questions for Guyer's reading. How can we reconcile the claim that the passion for freedom grounds morality with Kant's claim that the passions are morally corrosive? How can we reconcile Guyer's thesis that the freedom to set ends is the fundamental value in Kant's moral philosophy with Kant's focus on external freedom in his discussion of the passion for freedom? And if the passion for freedom cannot provide a ground for morality as it is, what can motivate its modification? But I have also shown that Kant's theory of the passions as a whole helps us provide answers to these questions. Kant discusses the passion for freedom along with the passion to use others as the ultimate means and its particular manifestations, the desires for honor, power, and possession. I have argued that the passions' defining feature in Kant's account is their social nature: they are aimed at other human beings as their object. This is because others' interference in our lives is the greatest threat to our freedom — so great in fact that any other threat is irrelevant by comparison — and because others' recognition, labor, and resources are the most valuable to the achievement of our ends — so valuable in fact that other means are irrelevant by comparison. I have argued that the tension between the passion for freedom and the particular passions is frustrating and spurs reflection: reason becomes engaged in thinking about the relationship between our own and others' ends. Where do they conflict? Where do they coincide? This reflection on the passions leads us to desire our own and others' freedom to set ends. On the picture I have suggested Kant's account has similarities both to Hume's account of the calm passions and to Rousseau's account of moral development based on amour-propre.

---

70 Guyer (2016), 202.

References

Borges, Maria (2021). "Passions and Evil in Kant's Philosophy." In *Kant on Emotions*, ed. by Mariannina Failla and Nuria Sánchez Madrid, Boston, 69–83.
Guyer, Paul (2007). "Naturalistic and Transcendental Moments in Kant's Moral Philosophy." *Inquiry. An Interdisciplinary Journal of Philosophy* 50 (5), 444–464.
Guyer, Paul (2016). *Virtues of Freedom*, New York.
Guyer, Paul (2000). *Kant on Freedom, Law and Happiness*, Cambridge.
Klemme, Heiner F. (2024). "Maximizing Freedom? Paul Guyer on the Value of Freedom and Reason in Kant." In *Kant on Freedom and Human Nature*, ed. by Luigi Filieri and Sofie Møller, New York.
Neuhouser, Frederick (2008). *Rousseau's Theodicy of Self-Love: Evil, Rationality, and the Drive for Recognition*, Oxford.
Rauscher, Frederick (2018). "Moral Realism and the Inner Value of the World." In *Kant on Freedom and Spontaneity*, ed. by Kate Moran, New York, 155–168.
Wood, Allen (2009). "Kant's Fourth Proposition: the unsociable sociability of human nature." In *Kant's Idea for a Universal History with a Cosmopolitan Aim*, ed. by Amélie Oksenberg Rorty and James Schmidt, Cambridge, 112–128.

Reed Winegar
The Beautiful and the Sublime in Kant's Early Natural Philosophy

Abstract: Paul Guyer's work has drawn much attention to the connection between aesthetics, morality, and teleology in Kant's *Critique of the Power of Judgment*. Indeed, Guyer has argued that Kant's recognition of such a connection in the 1780s provided the major impetus behind Kant's decision to write a third *Critique*. This essay aims to refine Guyer's interpretation of the development of Kant's views regarding this connection. It does so by focusing on the role of beauty and sublimity in Kant's early natural philosophy. These considerations demonstrate the need to refine Guyer's own interpretation in two ways. First, Guyer's claim that a connection between aesthetics and moral teleology was absent in Kant's thought prior to the third *Critique* needs to be moderated. Second, Kant's early conception of the sublime anticipates more of the third *Critique*'s account than Guyer recognizes.

Keywords: aesthetics, beauty, sublime, morality, teleology

1 Introduction

Paul Guyer's research has always emphasized the importance of Kant's aesthetics. Guyer's first book, *Kant and the Claims of Taste*,[1] quickly established itself as a classic in this area, and Kant's aesthetics remained a central feature of Guyer's subsequent work, evidenced by further books like *Kant and the Experience of Freedom*[2] and *Values of Beauty*.[3] Yet, while Guyer's *focus* on Kant's aesthetics has remained consistent, his *approach* to Kant's aesthetics has undergone significant change. Guyer himself has acknowledged the changes in his approach. Reflecting back on the character of his work after *Kant and the Claims of Taste*, Guyer writes:

> I did not find myself revising the interpretative framework of *Kant and the Claims of Taste* but placing it in a larger context or, more precisely, in two contexts: the historical context of Kant's relation to eighteenth-century aesthetics, and the philosophical context of its relation to Kant's

---

1 Guyer, Paul: *Kant and the Claims of Taste*. Cambridge, MA 1977.
2 Guyer, Paul: *Kant and the Experience of Freedom: Essays on Aesthetics and Morality*. Cambridge, New York, Melbourne 1993.
3 Guyer, Paul: *Values of Beauty: Historical Essays in Aesthetics*. New York 2005.

moral philosophy — which relation, I became increasingly convinced provided the fundamental motivation for Kant's excursion into aesthetic theory.[4]

As Guyer notes here, both Kant's 18th-century context and the third *Critique*'s consideration of the relationship between aesthetics and morality became increasingly central to his interpretation of Kant's aesthetics. Indeed, Guyer came to find Kant's chief motivation for writing a third *Critique* in Kant's appreciation of aesthetics' moral significance. Although Guyer advances aspects of this interpretation in various works, one finds an especially comprehensive treatment in his essay "Beauty, Freedom, and Morality: Kant's Lectures on Anthropology and the Development of his Aesthetic Theory."[5] This essay considers the development of Kant's aesthetics on the basis of Kant's anthropology lectures. Kant lectured on anthropology repeatedly over the decades, using the empirical psychology portion of Alexander Baumgarten's *Metaphysics* as a textbook. Baumgarten, who gave the term 'aesthetics' its modern meaning, discusses aesthetics within the empirical psychology section of his *Metaphysics*. Therefore, the lectures on anthropology provided Kant with ample opportunity to remark on issues in aesthetics. On the basis of Kant's anthropology lectures, Guyer draws the striking conclusion that Kant had already formulated most of the distinctive aspects of the third *Critique*'s mature aesthetic theory, such as the notion of an *a priori* principle of taste and the concept of a harmonious play of the cognitive faculties, in the 1770s, long before he ever envisioned writing a third *Critique*.

On Guyer's interpretation, Kant's ultimate decision in the late 1780s to write a third *Critique* was motivated less by new developments in Kant's aesthetic theory as such and more by Kant's increasing appreciation of aesthetics' significance for moral teleology. In particular, Guyer claims that Kant's increasing appreciation of the relationship between aesthetics and moral teleology provided the chief impetus for Kant's decision to write a third *Critique*:

> [...] what the lectures on anthropology show is that what the *Critique of Judgment* adds to all the elements of his aesthetic theory that were already in place by the mid-1780s is all and only those elements of the theory that reveal the teleological significance of the experience of beauty and of the existence of both natural and artistic beauty.[6]

According to Guyer, the suggestion of a relationship between aesthetics and moral teleology was absent in Kant's earlier thought and represents a key innovation of

---

4 Guyer, Paul: *Kant and the Experience of Freedom*.
5 Guyer, Paul: "Beauty, Freedom, and Morality."
6 Guyer: "Beauty, Freedom, and Morality," 165.

the third *Critique*. Referring to a well-known 1787 letter to Reinhold that contains Kant's reference to the work that would become the third *Critique*, Guyer writes, "What is unprecedented in Kant's work, however, is the suggestion in the letter to Reinhold that there is an intimate connection between aesthetics and teleology."[7] Indeed, Guyer takes this "intimate connection" to constitute Kant's primary motivation for writing a third *Critique*: "We can now see that it must be precisely this connection that finally enabled Kant to write the third *Critique* [...]".[8]

There are, of course, various questions that one might raise regarding Guyer's interpretation of the third *Critique*'s origins. For example, in the same 1787 letter to Reinhold mentioned above, Kant famously proclaims the discovery of an *a priori* principle of feeling.[9] One might be tempted to take this discovery of an *a priori* principle of feeling, rather than a specific concern with the significance of aesthetics for moral teleology, to have provided the primary impetus behind Kant's decision to write a third *Critique*. Guyer is aware of this objection. But he questions the extent to which Kant's 1787 conception of an *a priori* principle of feeling is really new, noting that "the lectures make it clear as no other sources do that Kant had in fact long considered the possibility and sometimes even asserted that there are *a priori* principles for the feeling of pleasure and displeasure, in the form of principles of taste."[10] Moreover, Guyer is reluctant to locate the third *Critique*'s primary origins in "a pedantic desire" for a complete taxonomy of *a priori* principles, suggesting instead that Kant's new appreciation of the relationship between aesthetics and moral teleology should be seen as "a much more profound and powerful motivation."[11]

My aim in this essay will not be to assess Guyer's proposal regarding the specific motivations that might have prompted Kant to write a third *Critique*. Rather, I want to focus on Guyer's related assessment of which aspects of the third *Critique* count as new innovations. In doing so, I will argue that Guyer's interpretation of the third *Critique*'s innovations regarding the relationships between aesthetic, morality, and teleology needs to be refined.[12] Guyer's interpretation draws heavily on Kant's anthropology lectures as well as many other aspects of Kant's corpus. Yet, there is one relevant area of Kant's thought to which Guyer's interpretation does

---

7 Ibid.
8 Ibid.
9 Br, AA 10: 514.
10 Guyer: "Beauty, Freedom, and Morality," 164.
11 Guyer, Paul: *A History of Modern Aesthetics, Volume 1: The Eighteenth-Century*. Cambridge, New York, Port Melbourne, New Delhi, Singapore 2014, 428.
12 I have discussed other aspects of the third *Critique*'s treatment of aesthetics' relationship to teleology in Winegar, Reed (2017), "Kant and Hutcheson on Aesthetics and Teleology" and Winegar, Reed (2021), "Kant's Antinomy of Taste and the Supersensible."

not pay serious attention — namely, Kant's early natural philosophy. I believe that a complete assessment of Kant's developing views regarding the relationship between aesthetics, morality, and teleology cannot afford to neglect this area of Kant's thought.[13] Based on a consideration of the aesthetic notions of the beautiful and the sublime in Kant's early natural philosophy, I will argue that Guyer's interpretation of the third *Critique*'s innovations regarding aesthetics, morality, and teleology needs to be amended in two respects. First, contrary to Guyer's suggestion, "an intimate connection between aesthetics and teleology" is not "unprecedented in Kant's work" prior to the 1787 letter to Reinhold.[14] In fact, aesthetics and teleology, including a kind of moral teleology, had long been intertwined in Kant's thought. Second, while Guyer notes that Kant refers to the sublime "only rarely in the anthropology lectures," we will see that the sublime played a significant role in Kant's early natural philosophy and that this early treatment of the sublime anticipates more of Kant's third *Critique* account than Guyer recognizes.[15] However, recognizing these points hardly undermines Guyer's overall contention that the third *Critique* introduces important innovations in Kant's thought regarding the connections between aesthetics, morality, and teleology. Rather, it simply helps put into relief the more specific aspects of those connections that should count as the third *Critique*'s true innovations.

---

13 The aesthetic dimensions of Kant's early natural philosophy have attracted minimal attention. In his recent book *The Origins of Kant's Aesthetics*, Robert Clewis notes in passing that the *Universal Natural History* refers to both sensory and intellectual beauty and that the book "contains what is likely Kant's earliest published statement on what he would later identify as the sublime;" Clewis, Robert (2023), *The Origins of Kant's Aesthetics*, 163. But he does not analyze these points in detail. Edward Kanterian acknowledges the "aesthetic element" in Kant's early natural philosophy, briefly relating Kant's early comments on awe and sublimity to Rudolf Otto's conception of the numinous; Kanterian, Edward (2018), *Kant, God, and Metaphysics: The Secret Thorn*, 95. However, Kanterian does not consider these points in relation to Kant's later positions in the third *Critique*. Susan Shell briefly suggests that the treatment of attraction and repulsion in the *Universal Natural History*'s treatment of the sun anticipates the third *Critique*'s notion of the dynamical sublime; Shell, Susan Meld (1996), *The Embodiment of Reason: Kant on Spirit, Generation, and Community*, 61–62. Manfred Kuehn notes that aesthetic concepts were often related to the 18th-century tradition of physico-theology, but he does not discuss their role in Kant's own early natural philosophy; Kuehn, Manfred (2001), *Kant: A Biography*, 345. Martin Schönfeld's sustained treatment of Kant's early natural philosophy (in Schönfeld, Martin (2000), *The Philosophy of the Young Kant*) largely ignores its aesthetic dimension.
14 Guyer: "Beauty, Freedom, and Morality," 165.
15 Guyer: "Beauty, Freedom, and Morality," 185.

2 Guyer on Aesthetics, Morality, and Teleology in the third *Critique*

Allow me to begin by presenting Guyer's interpretation in more detail. In assessing the origins of Kant's third *Critique*, Guyer recognizes that writing a "'critique of taste' was one of Kant's long-standing philosophical ambitions."[16] Kant's correspondence from the 1770s shows that Kant originally intended for the work that resulted in the *Critique of Pure Reason* to include a theory of taste.[17] However, the *Critique of Pure Reason* that appeared in 1781 does not contain any such theory. Moreover, in 1781, Kant did not envision writing any further critiques, aiming instead to develop a new metaphysics of morals and metaphysics of nature. Kant's decision to write a second critique, the *Critique of Practical Reason*, resulted from the process of revising the first *Critique* in preparation for the second edition of 1787.[18] Kant initially planned to publish the second edition with a new appendix containing a critique of pure practical reason, but this planned appendix eventually took on a life of its own, becoming the *Critique of Practical Reason*. Yet, Kant's plans for the *Critique of Pure Reason*'s second edition do not seem to have included any new plans for a critique of taste. Why then did Kant suddenly decide to write a third *Critique*, containing a "Critique of the Aesthetic Power of Judgment"?

As mentioned previously, we find Kant's first reference to the work that became the third *Critique* in a 1787 letter to Reinhold.[19] However, Guyer observes that Kant's "letter is initially confusing, for it suggests two different things as the key to Kant's project."[20] These are (1) Kant's discovery of an *a priori* principle of feeling and (2) teleology. As noted above, Guyer takes this suggestion of an intimate relationship between aesthetics and teleology to be "unprecedented" in Kant's prior thought and to have constituted Kant's primary motivation for writing a third *Critique*. What precisely are the connections between aesthetics and teleology that Guyer has in mind here? Although the third *Critique* provides a famous discussion of teleology in regards to organic generation, Guyer primarily interprets the letter to Reinhold in terms of Kant's *moral teleology*. Kant claims that the third *Critique* aims to help bridge the gulf between nature and freedom. In an often quoted passage, Kant writes:

---

16 Guyer: "Beauty, Freedom, and Morality," 163.
17 Br, AA 10: 514.24.
18 For a detailed overview of the second *Critique*'s origins, see Klemme, Heiner F. (2010), "The Origin and Aim of Kant's *Critique of Practical Reason*."
19 Br, AA 10: 513–516.
20 Guyer: "Beauty, Freedom, and Morality," 164.

> Now although there is an incalculable gulf fixed between the domain of the concept of nature, as the sensible, and the domain of the concept of freedom, as the supersensible, so that from the former to the latter (thus by means of the theoretical use of reason) no transition is possible, just as if there were so many different worlds, the first of which can have no influence on the second: yet the latter **should** have an influence on the former, namely the concept of freedom should make the end that is imposed by its laws real in the sensible world; and nature must consequently also be able to be conceived in such a way that the lawfulness of its form is at least in agreement with the possibility of the ends that are to be realized in it in accordance with the laws of freedom.[21]

According to Guyer, Kant's chief point here is that we need to be able to regard nature as amenable to the realization of our moral ends. Guyer observes that this point might initially seem puzzling. After all, the second *Critique*'s prior discussions of moral determination and the highest good might seem to have already shown that we can realize our moral ends in nature. What gulf between freedom and nature actually remains to be bridged?[22] Guyer answers this question by proposing that the second *Critique* advances *rational* arguments to justify the claim that we can realize our moral ends in nature, whereas the third *Critique* speaks to our needs as not only rational but also *sensible* beings, for whom the rational recognition of the possibility of realizing our moral ends in nature needs to be integrated with feeling and sensibility.[23]

Guyer notes several ways that the third *Critique* aims to speak to our needs as moral yet sensible beings. For instance, one point that the third *Critique* makes regarding the relationship between morality and sensibility is that aesthetic pleasure can help to provide a propaedeutic for moral feeling. Another point that the third *Critique* makes is that artworks can present moral ideas to sensibility. However, as Guyer recognizes, these suggestions are already found in earlier texts and are not entirely new in the third *Critique*.[24] Guyer seems, instead, to see the real innovations of the third *Critique* in its suggestion that our aesthetic experiences of beauty and

---

[21] KU, AA 05: 175.36–176.09: Ob nun zwar eine unübersehbare Kluft zwischen dem Gebiete des Naturbegriffs, als dem Sinnlichen, und dem Gebiete des Freiheitsbegriffs, als dem Übersinnlichen, befestigt ist, so daß von dem ersteren zum anderen (also vermittelst des theoretischen Gebrauchs der Vernunft) kein Übergang möglich ist, gleich als ob es so viel verschiedene Welten wären, deren erste auf die zweite keinen Einfluß haben kann: so *soll* doch diese auf jene einen Einfluß haben, nämlich der Freiheitsbegriff soll den durch seine Gesetze aufgegebenen Zweck in der Sinnenwelt wirklich machen; und die Natur muß folglich auch so gedacht werden können, daß die Gesetzmäßigkeit ihrer Form wenigstens zur Möglichkeit der in ihr zu bewirkenden Zwecke nach Freiheitsgesetzen zusammenstimme.
[22] Guyer: *Kant and the Experience of Freedom*, 28.
[23] Guyer: *Kant and the Experience of Freedom*, 30.
[24] Guyer: "Beauty, Freedom, and Morality," 181 and 184.

sublimity can make both our own moral freedom and nature's amenability to the realization of moral ends palpable to us. For instance, Guyer notes that Kant mentions the sublime "only rarely in the anthropology lectures, and then only in a limited way that suggests that even without proportion and symmetry the sheer magnitude of natural objects can affect the magnitude of our own feeling."[25] But in the third *Critique*'s "Analytic of the Sublime," Guyer notes that the aesthetic experience of the sublime makes "the independence of practical reason from mere nature palpable."[26] Similarly, Guyer takes the third *Critique* to introduce Kant's conception of beauty as a symbol of the morally-good, such that beauty provides a sensible, symbolic presentation "of the freedom of the will that is the basis of morality."[27] However, as noted above, Guyer is especially interested in the third *Critique*'s treatment of beauty's relationship to moral teleology, which he takes to constitute the third *Critique*'s most significant innovation: "The greatest innovation of the *Critique of the Power of Judgment*, however, is its unification of aesthetics into Kant's overarching vision of teleology."[28] Here Guyer emphasizes §42's discussion of the intellectual interest of beauty, where Kant famously indicates that natural beauty provides a hint of nature's amenability to the realization of moral ends. Guyer writes:

> Our deepest interest, of course, is that nature contain a ground for assuming its correspondence with the satisfaction of our moral interest, which is independent of all empirical interests but not of the interest of practical reason itself; but we can interpret nature's creation of beauty as evidence of its hospitality to our unselfish interest in morality as well. This conception of the intellectual interest in beauty does not depend upon an innovation in Kant's aesthetic theory itself, but rather in his development of the new moral teleology that is the deepest innovation of the *Critique of the Power of Judgment*.[29]

In a similar vein, Guyer also takes the third *Critique*'s novel characterization of genius as a gift of nature to indicate nature's amenability to the realization of moral ends, because it too illustrates that "the existence of artistic as well as natural beauty is evidence of the harmonious fit between nature and human objectives."[30] These, then, seem to be the main aspects of the relationship between aesthetics, morality, and teleology that Guyer takes to be distinctively new to Kant's thought in the third *Critique*.

---

25 Guyer: "Beauty, Freedom, and Morality," 185.
26 Ibid.
27 Ibid.
28 Guyer: "Beauty, Freedom, and Morality," 186.
29 Guyer: "Beauty, Freedom, and Morality," 187.
30 Guyer: "Beauty, Freedom, and Morality," 188.

3 Beauty and Teleology in Kant's Early Natural Philosophy

As noted above, my aim is neither to criticize Guyer's interpretation of the third *Critique* nor to criticize his interpretation of the anthropology lectures. Instead, I want to indicate a lacuna in Guyer's overall account of Kant's development. Namely, Guyer does not consider the role that aesthetic concepts like beauty and sublimity play in Kant's early natural philosophy. In the following, I will examine Kant's treatments of beauty and sublimity in his 1755 *Universal Natural History and Theory of the Heavens* and 1763 *The Only Possible Argument in Support of a Demonstration of the Existence of God*, i.e., the *Beweisgrund*. As I will aim to show, a proper consideration of these works will require us to moderate Guyer's claim that "an intimate connection between aesthetics and teleology" is "unprecedented in Kant's work" prior to the 1787 letter to Reinhold.[31] Moreover, while Guyer claims that Kant refers to the sublime "only rarely in the anthropology lectures," we will see that it played a pronounced role in Kant's early natural philosophy and that this early treatment of the sublime anticipates more of Kant's third *Critique* account than Guyer recognizes.[32] Appreciating these points will allow us to refine Guyer's picture of the third *Critique*'s novel innovations.

Guyer certainly acknowledges that Kant's general interest in questions regarding teleology are not new in the third *Critique*:

> By itself the idea that teleology might be a central part of philosophy is not new for Kant — in spite of his rejection of its traditional theological foundation in the argument from design, he had clearly been looking for a way to include teleology within his philosophy since his early work on *The Only Possible Basis for a Demonstration of the Existence of God* (1763).[33]

However, Guyer does not seem to acknowledge a relationship between beauty and teleology in Kant's early thought. This is unfortunate, for, such a relationship is evident in both the *Universal Natural History* and *Beweisgrund*. These two works were published eight years apart, but there is considerable overlap in a number of their topics and themes. Indeed, the *Beweisgrund* even contains an abridged version of the *Universal Natural History's* cosmogony, which Kant included because the bankruptcy of the *Universal Natural History's* publisher had frustrated the earlier work's distribution. For these reasons, I consider these two works together below.

---

31 Guyer: "Beauty, Freedom, and Morality," 165.
32 Guyer: "Beauty, Freedom, and Morality," 185.
33 Guyer: "Beauty, Freedom, and Morality," 165.

The *Universal Natural History* primarily aims to explain the formation of solar systems and galaxies. In this work, Kant positions his own cosmogony in relation to Newton's natural philosophy. On the one hand, Kant is deeply influenced by Newton, as evidenced by the book's full title: *Universal Natural History and Theory of the Heavens or Essay on the Constitution and the Mechanical Origin of the Whole Universe according to Newtonian Principles*.[34] On the other hand, the details of Kant's cosmogony differ significantly from Newton's own. Newton himself believed that particular features of our solar system (such as the fact that all of the planets are on a common orbital plane) could not be explained mechanically and must have required God's special intervention. Kant notes that for Newton "the direct hand of God had arranged this order without the application of the forces of nature."[35] In contrast to Newton, Kant aims to illustrate how our solar system, as well as the milky way and other solar systems and galaxies, could have arisen via merely mechanical laws from a prior state of chaotically swirling matter without a need for God's intervention.

It is important to recognize that part of the issue under consideration here was the formation of natural beauty. Indeed, Kant recognizes that people sympathetic to Newton's own position might worry that Kant's alternative explanation of "the beauty of the universe" tends towards atheism.[36] Voicing the fears of such potential critics, Kant writes:

> If the universe with all its order and beauty is merely an effect of matter left to its general laws of motion, if the blind mechanism of the powers of nature knows how to develop so magnificently and to such perfection all of its own accord: then the proof of the divine Author, which one derives from the sight of the beauty of the universe, is entirely stripped of its power, nature is sufficient in itself, divine government is superfluous, Epicure lives again in the middle of Christendom, and an unholy philosophy tramples faith under foot [...][37]

---

34 NTH, AA 01: 214: *Allgemeine Naturgeschichte und Theorie des Himmels oder Versuch von der Verfassung und dem mechanischen Ursprunge des ganzen Weltgebäudes, nach Newtonischen Grundsätzen abgehandelt.*
35 NTH, AA 01: 262.13–14: [...] die unmittelbare Hand Gottes habe diese Anordnung ohne die Anwendung der Kräfte der Natur ausgerichtet.
36 NTH, AA 01: 222.16 [...] der Schönheit des Weltgebäudes [...].
37 NTH, AA 01: 222.11–19: Wenn der Weltbau mit aller Ordnung und Schönheit nur eine Wirkung der ihren allgemeinen Bewegungsgesetzen überlassenen Materie ist, wenn die blinde Mechanik der Naturkräfte sich aus dem Chaos so herrlich zu entwickeln weiß und zu solcher Vollkommenheit von selber gelangt: so ist der Beweis des göttlichen Urhebers, den man aus dem Anblicke der Schönheit des Weltgebäudes zieht, völlig entkräftet, die Natur ist sich selbst genugsam, die göttliche Regierung ist unnöthig, Epikur lebt mitten im Christentume wieder auf, und eine unheilige Weltweisheit tritt den Glauben unter die Füße [...].

However, Kant pushes back against any such worry, maintaining that the existence of mechanical laws that allow matter to form itself into beautiful combinations out of chaos should actually be seen as evidence of God's existence:

> Matter, which is the original material of all things, is thus bound by certain laws, and if it is left free to these laws it must necessarily bring forth beautiful combinations. It is not at liberty to deviate from this plan of perfection. Since, therefore, it is subject to a most wise purpose, it must necessarily have been placed into such harmonious connections by a first cause that ruled over it, and *a God exists precisely because nature cannot behave in any way other than in a regular and orderly manner, even in chaos*.[38]

More specifically, Kant takes the fact that merely mechanical laws produce beautiful combinations to indicate that the essences of material things, which ground the mechanical laws, have their common ground in God. Kant writes:

> However, if one considers that nature and the eternal laws that are prescribed to substances for their interaction, are not a principle independent and necessary without God, that precisely because of the fact that it shows so much correspondence and order in what it produces through universal laws, we can see that the essences of all things must have their common origin in a certain primitive being and that for this reason they reveal many reciprocal relationships and much harmony because their properties have their source in a single highest understanding, whose sage idea designed them in constant proportions and implanted in them that ability by which they produce much beauty, much order in the state of activity if left to themselves, if, I say, one considers this, then nature will appear to us more dignified than it is commonly regarded and one will expect from its unfolding nothing but correspondence, nothing but order.[39]

---

[38] NTH, AA 01: 228.03–11: Die Materie, die der Urstoff aller Dinge ist, ist also an gewisse Gesetze gebunden, welchen sie frei überlassen nothwendig schöne Verbindungen hervorbringen muß. Sie hat keine Freiheit von diesem Plane der Vollkommenheit abzuweichen. Da sie also sich einer höchst weisen Absicht unterworfen befindet, so muß sie nothwendig in solche übereinstimmende Verhältnisse durch eine über sie herrschende erste Ursache versetzt worden sein, und es ist *ein Gott eben deswegen, weil die Natur auch selbst im Chaos nicht anders als regelmäßig und ordentlich verfahren kann*.

[39] NTH, AA 01: 332.20–35: Wenn man aber erwägt, daß die Natur und die ewigen Gesetze welche den Substanzen zu ihrer Wechselwirkung vorgeschrieben sind, kein selbständiges und ohne Gott nothwendiges Principium sei, daß eben dadurch, weil sie so viel Übereinstimmung und Ordnung in demjenigen zeigt, was sie durch allgemeine Gesetze hervorbringt, zu ersehen ist, daß die Wesen aller Dinge in einem gewissen Grundwesen ihren gemeinschaftlichen Ursprung haben müssen, und daß sie darum lauter gewechselte Beziehungen und lauter Harmonie zeigen, weil ihre Eigenschaften in einem einzigen höchsten Verstande ihre Quelle haben, dessen weise Idee sie in durchgängigen Beziehungen entworfen und ihnen diejenige Fähigkeit eingepflanzt hat, dadurch sie lauter Schönheit, lauter Ordnung in dem ihnen selbst gelassenen Zustande ihrer Wirksamkeit

Kant elaborates on and refines this idea in the *Beweisgrund*. This work is best known today for its *a priori* argument of God's existence. This argument, known as the modal argument, conceives of God as the ground of all possibility, arguing from the fact that things are possible to the existence of God. However, Kant spends much of the *Beweisgrund* relating this *a priori* argument's conception of God as the ground of possibility to natural philosophy. In light of the above passage from the *Universal Natural History*, this is not surprising, for Kant takes the *Beweisgrund*'s conception of God as the ground of all possibility entail the *Universal Natural History*'s conception of God as the common ground of the essences of all things. In regards to natural philosophy, the *Beweisgrund* pursues this picture in more detail as follows.

To begin, Kant notes that the existence of all finite things is contingent and that all finite things consequently depend on God's will for their creation. However, amongst created things, there are two types of natural order, which correspond to different ways that natural order can depend on God. These are contingent natural order and necessary natural order. Cases of contingent order depend on God's special institutions. Kant's primary example of such order is the order found in plants and animal bodies: "The creatures of the plant- and animal-kingdoms everywhere offer the most admirable examples of a unity which is at once contingent and yet in harmony with great wisdom."[40] According to Kant, merely mechanical laws cannot explain the formation of plant and animal bodies. The formation of such bodies relies, instead, on some special divine institution. Second, there is necessary natural order. This is order that arises from the essences of existing things without requiring any special institutions. Contrary to people like Newton, Kant takes the order of the solar system to be an instance of necessary natural order. Once God creates matter, it will operate according to merely mechanical laws and, in doing so, will form itself into solar systems like our own. However, these mechanical laws are grounded on the essence of matter, and the fact that the essences of things are even able to give rise to such order results from the fact that these essences depend on God, conceived as the ground of all possibility. There are, consequently, two different ways to argue from the order of nature to the existence of God. First, we can argue from the contingent order of nature to the existence of God, who has willed to specially

---

hervorbringen, wenn man, sage ich, dieses erwägt, so wird die Natur uns würdiger, als sie gemeiniglich angesehen wird, erscheinen, und man wird von ihren Auswickelungen nichts, als Übereinstimmung, nichts als Ordnung erwarten.

40 BDG, AA 02: 107.14–16: Die Geschöpfe des Pflanzen- und Thierreichs bieten durchgängig die bewundernswürdigste Beispiele einer zufälligen, aber mit großer Weisheit übereinstimmenden Einheit dar.

institute such order. Second, we can argue from the necessary order of nature to God who, as the ground of all possibility, grounds the essences of things.

Here we need to be careful. Initially, one might think that the distinction between these two types of order amounts to a distinction between order that involves divine teleology and order that does not involve any divine teleology. But this would be mistaken. While the case of contingent order clearly involves divine teleology, the case of necessary natural order does as well. In particular, Kant maintains that God chooses which particular things to create. This choice of particular things is based on God's recognition that the essences of these things will lead them to produce some specific natural order. Therefore, there is still a moment of divine choice and, correspondingly, divine teleology at play in the case of the necessary order of nature.

As we can see from the various passages quoted above, Kant's early natural philosophy closely associates beauty with concepts like order and harmony, often mentioning them together in a single breath, such that the *Beweisgrund*'s general discussion of natural order bears directly on natural beauty. In the *Beweisgrund*, Kant claims that beauty can belong either to the contingent order of nature or to the necessary order of nature. For instance, Kant refers to "the contingent beauties of nature."[41] But he also repeatedly emphasizes the beauty, including that of the solar system and galaxies, that results from merely mechanical laws and, therefore, belongs to the necessary order of nature. Additionally, Kant claims that beautiful geometric relations belong to the necessary order of nature, arousing emotions "in a manner similar to or even more sublime than that in which the contingent beauties of nature stir the feelings."[42] On Kant's view, these beautiful geometric relations obtain not merely because God has created space but because the very essence of space is grounded in God, as the ground of all possibility.

Kant takes all of these different types of natural beauty to provide evidence for the existence of God. Indeed, the *Beweisgrund* emphasizes the importance of arguments from the order, harmony, and beauty of nature to the existence of God. As noted previously, the *Beweisgrund* holds that we can demonstrate God's existence *a priori*. However, it also emphasizes the importance of sensible confirmation for rational *a priori* arguments, especially in a case of such significance as the existence of God, which bears on the momentous ethical concern of one's eternal happiness: "It is unlikely that anyone would venture his whole happiness upon the pretended

---

[41] BDG, AA 02: 95.29: [...] die zufällige Schönheiten der Natur [...].
[42] BDG, AA 02: 95.29–30: [...] auf eine ähnliche oder erhabnere Art wie die zufällige Schönheiten der Natur rühren. We might note that the beauty of geometric relations here seems to be a kind of intellectual beauty.

correctness of a metaphysical proof, especially if that proof were opposed by vivid objections which appealed to the senses."[43] Kant maintains that arguments from the order, harmony, and beauty of nature appeal to the senses and, as such, produce a conviction "so firm and unshakeable as to be unperturbed by any threats to it posed by syllogistic discourses and distinctions."[44] Moreover, Kant insists that this conviction is morally valuable because it helps to produce virtuous behavior in people. Referring to the conviction produced even by the common understanding's consideration of the contingent order of nature, Kant writes: "This conviction, in so far as it is supposed to be sufficient to produce virtuous behavior, that is to say, is supposed to be morally certain, can be arrived at by means of the ordinary concepts of the understanding."[45]

With these points in mind, we can see that an intimate connection between aesthetics and teleology, including moral teleology, was hardly unprecedented in Kant's thought prior to the third *Critique*. Kant's conception of the beauty that results from the necessary order of nature already anticipates to some extent the third *Critique*'s claims regarding the production of beauty via merely mechanical laws in §58's discussion of the idealism of purposiveness. But in Kant's early thought, the production of beauty via the necessary order of nature still relies on God's choice of which particular things (with their particular essences) to create and, thus, involves divine teleology; this point might be regarded as a partial forerunner of Kant's claim in the "Critique of the Teleological Power of Judgment" that, once we reflectively adopt a teleological perspective on nature as a whole, we can reflectively judge even beautiful objects produced by mechanical laws as ends.[46] Moreover, in partial anticipation of the third *Critique*'s attempt to bridge the gulf between nature and freedom, Kant already recognized the need to make rational thoughts sensibly palpable and claimed that the consideration of natural beauty can help us in this regard. Kant even regarded the experience of natural beauty as morally significant, given that it leads to a conviction in God's existence that both promotes virtuous behavior and offers a promise of future happiness, partially

---

43 BDG, AA 02: 118.04–07: Schwerlich würde wohl jemand seine ganze Glückseligkeit auf die angemaßte Richtigkeit eines metaphysischen Beweises wagen, vornehmlich wenn ihm lebhafte sinnliche Überredungen entgegen ständen.
44 BDG, AA 02: 118.08–10: [...] so gesetzt und unerschütterlich, daß sie keine Gefahr von Schlußreden und Unterscheidungen besorgt [...].
45 BDG, AA 02: 116.26–28: [...] es sind zu dieser Überzeugung, so fern sie zum tugendhaften Verhalten hinlänglich, das ist, moralisch gewiß sein soll, die gemeine Begriffe des Verstandes hinreichend.
46 KU, AA 05: 380:13–25. One might wonder how this aspect of Kant's view squares with his conception of beauty in terms of purposiveness without purpose, but I am not able to consider that further issue here.

anticipating the third *Critique*'s claim that people's consideration of natural beauty has "served admirably to strengthen that idea [...]" of God as the ground of the highest good.⁴⁷

Yet, one thing missing from these early connections between aesthetics, teleology, and morality is any suggestion that beauty has some particularly special role to play in contrast to other related notions like order and harmony. I would suggest, then, that we amend Guyer's somewhat sweeping claim that a connection between aesthetics and teleology, including moral teleology, is unprecedented in Kant's thought prior to the third *Critique*. Rather, the truly innovative aspect of the third *Critique*'s approach to this relationship concerns the way in which Kant's mature aesthetic theory conceives of beauty specifically as providing a hint of nature's amenability to the realization of moral ends in the natural world. More specifically, Kant claims in §42 that we take a moral interest in natural beauty, because the precise way in which the pleasure of natural beauty parallels moral feeling provides a hint of nature's amenability to moral ends.⁴⁸ As Kant puts the point:

> But since it also interests reason that the ideas (for which it produces an immediate interest in the moral feeling) also have objective reality, i.e., that nature should at least show some trace or give a sign that it contains in itself some sort of ground for assuming a lawful correspondence of its products with our satisfaction that is independent of all interest [...] reason must take an interest in every manifestation in nature of a correspondence similar to this [...].⁴⁹

This more specific claim, which relies on particular aspects of Kant's critical moral theory as well as Kant's mature aesthetic theory, does not appear anywhere in Kant's early natural philosophy.

---

47 KU, AA 05: 459.04.
48 One might take R 1820a from the 1770s to foreshadow this idea: "Beautiful things indicate that the human being belongs in the world. [Die Schöne Dinge zeigen an, daß der Mensch in die Welt passe.] [...]" (Refl, AA 16: 127). But this *Reflexion* does not actually mention morality.
49 KU, AA 05: 300.23–33: "Da es aber die Vernunft auch interessirt, daß die Ideen (für die sie im moralischen Gefühle ein unmittelbares Interesse bewirkt) auch objective Realität haben, d. i. daß die Natur wenigstens eine Spur zeige, oder einen Wink gebe, sie enthalte in sich irgend einen Grund, eine gesetzmäßige Übereinstimmung ihrer Producte zu unserm von allem Interesse unabhängigen Wohlgefallen [...] anzunehmen: so muß die Vernunft an jeder Äußerung der Natur von einer dieser ähnlichen Übereinstimmung ein Interesse nehmen [...].

4 The Sublime in Kant's Early Natural Philosophy

The sublime also plays a pronounced role in Kant's early natural philosophy. Kant explicitly refers to a "sublime view" of the cosmos, and many passages employ multiple tropes related to the 18th-century's general conception of the sublime, such as astonishment, eternity, hiddenness, infinity, the night sky, nobility, profundity, stillness, and so on.[50] Consider, for example, the closing lines of the *Universal Natural History*:

> Indeed, when one has filled one's mind with such observations and the preceding ones, the view of the starry sky on a clear night gives one a kind of pleasure that only noble souls feel. In the universal stillness of nature and the calmness of the senses the immortal spirit's hidden faculty of cognition speaks an ineffable language and provides undeveloped concepts that can certainly be felt but not described. If, among the thinking creatures of this planet, there are any despicable beings who, in spite of all the delights with which so great an object can attract them, are yet in a position to tie themselves firmly to the service of vanity, how unfortunate is this sphere that it has been able to bring up such miserable creatures! But how fortunate is it, on the other hand, because under the most acceptable of conditions a way has been opened for it to attain bliss and sublimity [*Hoheit*] that is exalted [*erhaben*] infinitely far above the benefits that the most advantageous arrangement of nature can attain in all celestial bodies![51]

It is, however, important to acknowledge that the line between the beautiful and the sublime is not always sharp in Kant's early writings. He sometimes seems to associate them with one another, such as when he writes: "By its immeasurable magnitude and by the infinite diversity and beauty that shines forth from it on all

---

50 NTH, AA 01: 253.20 [...] erhabene Vorstellung [...]
51 NTH, AA 01: 367.26–368.06: In der That wenn man mit solchen Betrachtungen und mit den vorhergehenden sein Gemüth erfüllt hat: so giebt der Anblick eines bestirnten Himmels bei einer heitern Nacht eine Art des Vergnügens, welches nur edle Seelen empfinden. Bei der allgemeinen Stille der Natur und der Ruhe der Sinne redet das verborgene Erkenntnißvermögen des unsterblichen Geistes eine unnennbare Sprache und giebt unausgewickelte Begriffe, die sich wohl empfinden, aber nicht beschreiben lassen. Wenn es unter den denkenden Geschöpfen dieses Planeten niederträchtige Wesen giebt, die ungeachtet aller Reizungen, womit ein so großer Gegenstand sie anlocken kann, dennoch im Stande sind, sich fest an die Dienstbarkeit der Eitelkeit zu heften: wie unglücklich ist diese Kugel, daß sie so elende Geschöpfe hat erziehen können! Wie glücklich aber ist sie andererseits, da ihr unter den allerannehmungswürdigsten Bedingungen ein Weg eröffnet ist, zu einer Glückseligkeit und Hoheit zu gelangen welche unendlich weit über die Vorzüge erhaben ist, die die allervortheilhafteste Einrichtung der Natur in allen Weltkörpern erreichen kann!

sides, the universe puts us into silent astonishment."[52] One might take this to be an example of what Kant in his 1764 *Observations on the Feeling of the Beautiful and Sublime*, calls the magnificent sublime, where a sublime prospect includes a large array of beautiful objects.[53] But Kant also sometimes refers to the sublime as itself a type of beauty, such as when he writes: "However, the designation 'infinity' is beautiful and genuinely aesthetic. Extension beyond all numerical stirs the emotions, and, in virtue of a certain embarrassment which it causes, it fills the soul with astonishment."[54] Yet, given that a sharp distinction between the beautiful and the sublime arose only gradually in the 18th-century, Kant's early terminology is not unusual in this respect, and we can identify elements of Kant's early natural philosophy that clearly belong to the discourse of sublimity.[55]

Why exactly does Kant take his early picture of the universe to be sublime? To answer this question, we need to describe Kant's early picture in slightly more detail. As outlined above, the *Universal Natural History* aims to illustrate the formation of solar systems and galaxies by means of merely mechanical laws. But Kant's more detailed theory is as follows. At an earlier stage, the universe consisted of swirling matter distributed throughout infinite space. Given merely mechanical laws, this matter started to clump together into bodies, forming a large body around which other bodies rotated. This process continued, such that new solar systems and galaxies were formed. In fact, this process still continues today, with new solar systems and galaxies constantly being formed from the chaotic swirls of matter at the edge of the ordered cosmos. Yet, the same mechanical laws that give rise to solar systems and galaxies will also ultimately lead to their destruction. But given that solar systems and galaxies will arise from chaotic swirling matter via merely

---

52 NTH, AA 01: 306.16–18: Das Weltgebäude setzt durch seine unermeßliche Größe und durch die unendliche Mannigfaltigkeit und Schönheit, welche aus ihm von allen Seiten hervorleuchten, in ein stilles Erstaunen.

53 Clewis, *The Origins of Kant's Aesthetics*, 163. Other 18th-century authors also allow for versions of this kind of sublimity. For instance, Burke, Edmund (2008, [1757]), *A Philosophical Enquiry into the Sublime and the Beautiful*, 77, makes a similar point, referring specifically to beautiful stars in the night sky: "A great profusion of things, which are splendid or valuable in themselves is *magnificent*. The starry heaven, though it occurs so frequently to our view, never fails to excite an idea of grandeur."

54 BDG, AA 02: 154.19–22: Die Benennung der Unendlichkeit ist gleichwohl schön und eigentlich ästhetisch. Die Erweiterung über alle Zahlbegriffe rührt und setzt die Seele durch eine gewisse Verlegenheit in Erstaunen.

55 Monk, Samuel H. (1960 [1935]), *The Sublime: A Study of Critical Theories in XVIII-Century England*, provides a discussion of this history, identifying Addison as the first person to clearly distinguish the sublime from the beautiful. Clewis, *The Origins of Kant's Aesthetics*, 157 notes that Baumgarten still regarded the sublime as a type of beauty.

mechanical laws, the chaos resulting from this destruction will lead in turn to the formation of new solar systems and galaxies, replacing the old ones. The infinite cosmos is, therefore, in a constant state of formation and destruction. Note that this picture of the universe contains the two elements that become key to the third *Critique*'s later distinction between the mathematical and dynamical sublime: namely, infinity and destructive power. Kant does not yet draw a clear distinction between the mathematical and dynamical sublime, but he definitely relates both these two elements to the feeling of sublimity. In regards to infinity, he writes:

> If the magnitude of a planetary system in which the earth is as a grain of sand and scarcely noticeable puts our reason into a state of wonderment, then with what amazement are we delighted when we contemplate the infinite multitude of worlds and systems that constitute the sum of the milky way; but how much does this amazement increase when one becomes aware that all these immeasurable orders of stars in turn are the unit of a number whose end we do not know, and which is perhaps just as inconceivably great as these and yet is in turn only the unit of a new combination of numbers.[56]

And Kant relates his conception of the universe as undergoing constant formation and destruction to the general notion of the sublime, writing: "[...] then the mind that contemplates all this sinks into a profound astonishment [...]"[57]

In the third *Critique*, Kant famously claims that the aesthetic experience of the sublime leads from our observation of enormous magnitude or destructive power to a consideration of our own reason. However, Kant's position differs in the earlier *Universal Natural History* and *Beweisgrund*. In the *Universal Natural History* he claims that our profound astonishment leads to the thought of God:

> [...] then the mind that contemplates all this sinks into a profound astonishment; and yet still unsatisfied with this so great object, whose transience cannot satisfy the soul sufficiently, he

---

[56] NTH, AA 01: 256.02–11: Wenn die Größe eines planetischen Weltbaues, darin die Erde als ein Sandkorn kaum bemerkt wird, den Verstand in Verwunderung setzt, mit welchem Erstaunen wird man entzückt, wenn man die unendliche Menge Welten und Systemen ansieht, die den Inbegriff der Milchstraße erfüllen; allein wie vermehrt sich dieses Erstaunen, wenn man gewahr wird, daß alle diese unermeßliche Sternordnungen wiederum die Einheit von einer Zahl machen deren Ende wir nicht wissen, und die vielleicht eben so wie jene unbegreiflich groß und doch wiederum noch die Einheit einer neuen Zahlverbindung ist.
[57] NTH, AA 01: 321.21–22: [...] so versenkt sich der Geist, der alles dieses überdenkt, in ein tiefes Erstaunen [...]

wishes to get to know at close quarters that being whose understanding is the source of the light which spreads over all of nature as though from one centre point.[58]

In this general context, the *Beweisgrund* specifically singles out the sublimity of God's all-sufficiency:[59]

> The sum of all these reflections leads us to the concept of the Supreme Being. This Supreme Being embraces within itself everything which can be thought by man, when he, a creature made of dust, dares to cast a spying eye behind the curtain which veils from mortal eyes the mysteries of the inscrutable. God is all-sufficient. Whatever exists, whether it be possible or actual, is only something in so far as it is given through Him. If it be permitted to translate the communings of the Infinite with Himself into human language, we may imagine God addressing Himself in these terms: *I am from eternity to eternity: apart from me there is nothing, except it be through me*. This thought, of all thoughts the most sublime, is still widely neglected, and mostly not considered at all.[60]

Here Kant portrays God as all-sufficient, such that God does not depend on anything else, while all other things, including all possibilities, depend on God. As all-sufficient, God possesses a supreme type of independence. We should note Kant also refers to God in the above passage as the Infinite. But Kant clarifies that this is itself a poetic reference to God's all-sufficiency. He observes that the "concept of divine *all-sufficiency*, expanded to include all that is possible or real, is a far more appropriate expression for designating the supreme perfection of the Divine Being

---

58 NTH, AA 01: 321.21–26: [...] so versenkt sich der Geist, der alles dieses überdenkt, in ein tiefes Erstaunen; aber annoch mit diesem so großen Gegenstande unzufrieden, dessen Vergänglichkeit die Seele nicht gnugsam zufrieden stellen kann, wünscht er dasjenige Wesen von nahem kennen zu lernen, dessen Verstand, dessen Größe die Quelle desjenigen Lichtes ist, das sich über die gesammte Natur gleichsam als aus einem Mittelpunkte ausbreitet.

59 We might note that the following passage seems to anticipate the third *Critique*'s reference to the goddess Isis: "Perhaps nothing more sublime has ever been said, or any thought more sublimely expressed, than in the inscription over the temple of **Isis** (Mother **Nature**): 'I am all that is, that was, and that will be, and my veil no mortal has removed [Vielleicht ist nie etwas Erhabneres gesagt, oder ein Gedanke erhaben ausgedruckt worden, als in jener Aufschrift über dem Tempel der Isis (der Mutter *Natur*): 'Ich bin alles, was da ist, was da war, und was da sein wird, und meinen Schleier hat kein Sterblicher aufgedeckt]." (KU 05: 316.31–34).

60 BDG, AA 02: 151.05–15: Die Summe alle dieser Betrachtungen führt uns auf einen Begriff von dem höchsten Wesen, der alles in sich faßt, was man nur zu gedenken vermag, wenn Menschen, aus Staube gemacht, es wagen ausspähende Blicke hinter den Vorgang zu werfen, der die Geheimnisse des Unerforschlichen für erschaffene Augen verbirgt. Gott ist allgenugsam. Was da ist, es sei möglich oder wirklich, das ist nur etwas, in so fern es durch ihn gegeben ist. Eine menschliche Sprache kann den Unendlichen so zu sich selbst reden lassen: *Ich bin von Ewigkeit zu Ewigkeit, außer mir ist nichts, ohne in so fern es durch mich etwas ist*. Dieser Gedanke, der erhabenste unter allen, ist noch sehr vernachlässigt, oder mehrenteils gar nicht berührt worden.

than the concept of the *infinite*, which is commonly employed. For no matter how this latter concept be interpreted, its fundamental meaning is manifestly mathematical."[61] Here Kant notes that we cannot apply the mathematical concept 'infinite' to God in rigor, instead the term 'all-sufficient' (allgenugsam) "satisfies the demands of logical rigour to a greater degree."[62] But Kant still permits the use of the term 'infinite' here because (to repeat a passage quoted previously) it is "beautiful and genuinely aesthetic" as it "stirs the emotions, and in virtue of a certain embarrassment which it causes, it fills the soul with astonishment."[63] In other words, Kant describes God as infinite because that description helps to elicit a feeling of the sublimity of God's all-sufficiency — that is, of God's absolute independence.

While Kant here emphasizes a move from our observation of the cosmos to the thought of God's all-sufficiency, he also takes our observation of the cosmos to lead to the thought of our own immortality. More specifically, the destructive power of nature at play in the cosmos gives rise to a consideration of the transience of things and to our own natural mortality. This thought leads in turn to a consideration of the soul's immortality: "When the shackles that hold us to the vanity of creatures have fallen off at the moment that has been determined for the transfiguration of our being, then the immortal spirit, liberated from dependence on finite things, and in the company of the infinite being, will find the enjoyment of true happiness."[64] 18th-century authors often associated immortality with the sublime, as in the case of Edward Young's influential poem *The Complaint: or Night Thoughts on Life, Death, and Immortality*. In the *Observations*, Kant himself states in passing that "the immortality of our soul" possesses "a certain sublimity and dignity," but he does not stop to explain why.[65] However, in the *Universal Natural History*, Kant associates the sublime with the notion of the immortal soul's liberation from a dependence on finite things:

---

61 BDG, AA 02: 154.04–09: Es ist auch dieser über alles Mögliche und Wirkliche erweiterte Begriff der göttlichen *Allgenugsamkeit* ein viel richtigerer Ausdruck, die größte Vollkommenheit dieses Wesens zu bezeichnen, als der des *Unendlichen*, dessen man sich gemeiniglich bedient. Denn ob man diesen letztern zwar auslegen kann, wie man will, so ist er seiner eigentlichen Bedeutung nach doch offenbar mathematisch.
62 BDG, AA 02: 154.23: [...] der logischen Richtigkeit mehr angemessen.
63 BDG, AA 02: 154.20–22: [...] schön und eigentlich ästhetisch [...], [...] rührt und setzt die Seele durch eine gewisse Verlegenheit in Erstaunen.
64 NTH, AA 01: 322.06–11: Wenn dann die Fesseln, welche uns an die Eitelkeit der Kreaturen geknüpft halten, in dem Augenblicke, welcher zu der Verwandlung unsers Wesens bestimmt worden, abgefallen sind, so wird der unsterbliche Geist, von der Abhängigkeit der endlichen Dinge befreit, in der Gemeinschaft mit dem unendlichen Wesen den Genuß der wahren Glückseligkeit finden.
65 BGSE, AA 02: 215.19–20: [...] der Unsterblichkeit unserer Seele [...] eine gewisse Erhabenheit und Würde.

> With what kind of reverence does not the soul have to regard even its own being, when it considers that it is to survive all these changes [...] O happy, if among the tumult of the elements and the ruins of nature, it is always positioned at a height from which it can see the devastations that frailty causes the things the world to rush past under its feet, so to speak! [...] The changeable scenes of nature are not capable of disturbing the peace of happiness of a spirit that has been raised to such heights... [*zu solcher Höhe erhoben ist*][66]

Here Kant refers to the soul's sublimity in terms of an elevation above the destructive power of nature, associating this elevation with a feeling of reverence [*Ehrfurcht*] to connote respect for the sublimity of one's immortal soul. These remarks further illustrate the extent to which Kant's early thought associates the sublime with independence, in this case the soul's independence from nature.[67] This concept of independence is the common link between Kant's characterizations of both God's all-sufficiency and the soul's immortality as sublime.

Guyer's interpretation of the anthropology lectures seems to suggest that most of the elements of Kant's mature theory of the sublime, such as the distinction between the mathematical and dynamical sublime, the relationship between reason and imagination, and the relevance of our own moral freedom, are late additions to Kant's aesthetic theory. However, our consideration of the sublime in Kant's early natural philosophy allows us to refine Guyer's interpretation. Although Kant's early thought does not draw a clear terminological distinction between the mathematical and dynamical sublime, it clearly deals with the sublime in the context of both infinity and destructive power.[68] Moreover, although Kant's early treatment of the sublime discusses neither theoretical nor practical reason's independence from sensibility (which is not surprising, given that Kant had not yet developed his critical conception of pure reason), it does already relate the notion of the sublime to the concept of independence, including our own independence from nature. The major shift in Kant's thought here between his early natural philosophy and the

---

66 NTH, 01: 321.26–322.19: Mit welcher Art der Ehrfurcht muß nicht die Seele sogar ihr eigen Wesen ansehen, wenn sie betrachtet, daß sie noch alle diese Veränderungen überleben soll [...] O glücklich, wenn sie unter dem Tumult der Elemente und den Trümmern der Natur jederzeit auf eine Höhe gesetzt ist, von da sie die Verheerungen, die die hinfälligkeit den Dingen der Welt verursacht, gleichsam unter ihren Füßen kann vorbei rauschen sehen! [...] Die veränderlichen Scenen der Natur vermögen nicht, den Ruhestand der Glückseligkeit eines Geistes zu verrücken, der einmal zu solcher Höhe erhoben ist.
67 Denker, Alfred (2001), "The Vocation of the Human Being: Kant's Early Practical Philosophy, 1747–1765," 132 briefly notes the importance of the soul's independence here but relates it simply to Kant's ethical, rather than aesthetic, concerns.
68 One might note that the *Observations* also refer to cases of infinity and power as sublime. But the central importance of these two specific elements is less clearly pronounced there.

third *Critique* seems to concern the specific type of independence at play, such that Kant moves from an emphasis on God's all-sufficiency and the independence of our immortal souls to a new emphasis on the independence of theoretical and practical reason from sensibility.[69]

5 Conclusion

Paul Guyer's work on Kant's aesthetics has deeply influenced our contemporary understanding of the third *Critique*. Over time, Guyer's approach to Kant's aesthetics has come to focus increasingly on the moral significance of Kant's aesthetics. I believe that Guyer is correct to highlight the importance of this aspect of Kant's third *Critique*, even if I have declined to weigh in on the question of whether it constituted Kant's primary motivation for writing the book. My main aim has been to illustrate that Guyer's interpretation of Kant's development should be supplemented by a serious consideration of Kant's treatment of aesthetic concepts like beauty and sublimity in his early natural philosophy. In doing so, I have argued that we need to refine Guyer's interpretation of the extent to which the relationship between aesthetics and teleology is new to Kant's thought in the third *Critique*. Additionally, I have attempted to show that the sublime plays a pronounced role in Kant's early natural philosophy and that Kant's early conception of the sublime already employs a concept of independence that foreshadows aspects of the third *Critique*'s own theory. I hope, however, that these refinements might be seen as friendly amendments to Guyer's overall interpretation that help put into relief the specifically new ways in which the third *Critique* comes to relate aesthetics, morality, and teleology to one another.[70]

---

69 Clewis, *The Origins of Kant's Aesthetics*, 178 and Shell, *The Embodiment of Reason*, 62 suggest that Kant shifts from a more theologically-oriented theory of the sublime to an emphasis on reason in the third *Critique*. But they do not draw attention to the specific importance of all-sufficiency as a kind of independence in Kant's early thought, and they do not analyze the sublimity of immortality in Kant's early thought. We should also note that the third *Critique* does not dismiss the concept of theological sublimity entirely; see KU, AA 05: 108.35. But the question of how exactly the third *Critique*'s references to God's sublimity relate to its mature theory of the sublime is not one that I can pursue here.
70 I would like to thank Robert Clewis for comments on this paper.

References

Burke, Edmund (2008 [1757]). *A Philosophical Enquiry into the Sublime and the Beautiful*, Milton Park, New York.
Clewis, Robert (2023). *The Origins of Kant's Aesthetics*, Cambridge, New York, Melbourne, New Delhi, Singapore.
Denker, Alfred (2001). "The Vocation of the Human Being: Kant's Early Practical Philosophy, 1747–1765." In *New Essays on the Precritical Kant*, ed. by Tom Rockmore, Amherst, NY.
Guyer, Paul (1977). *Kant and the Claims of Taste*, Cambridge, MA.
Guyer, Paul (1993). *Kant and the Experience of Freedom: Essays on Aesthetics and Morality*, Cambridge, New York, Melbourne.
Guyer, Paul (2005a). *Values of Beauty: Historical Essays in Aesthetics*, New York.
Guyer, Paul (2005b). "Beauty, Freedom, and Morality: Kant's Lectures on Anthropology and the Development of his Aesthetic Theory." In *Values of Beauty: Historical Essays in Aesthetics*, New York.
Guyer, Paul (2014). *A History of Modern Aesthetics, Volume 1: The Eighteenth-Century*, Cambridge, New York, Port Melbourne, New Delhi, Singapore.
Kanterian, Edward (2018). *Kant, God, and Metaphysics: The Secret Thorn*, Milton Park, New York.
Klemme, Heiner F. (2010). "The Origin and Aim of Kant's Critique of Practical Reason." In *Kant's Critique of Practical Reason: A Critical Guide*, ed. by Andrews Reath and Jens Timmermann, Cambridge, New York, Melbourne, Madrid, Capetown, Singapore, São Paulo, Delhi, Mexico City.
Kuehn, Manfred (2001). *Kant: A Biography*, Cambridge, New York, Melbourne, Madrid, Cape Town.
Monk, Samuel H. (1960 [1935]). *The Sublime: A Study of Critical Theories in XVIII-Century England*, Ann Arbor.
Schönfeld, Martin (2000). *The Philosophy of the Young Kant: The Precritical Project*, New York.
Shell, Susan Meld (1996). *The Embodiment of Reason: Kant on Spirit, Generation, and Community*, Chicago.
Winegar, Reed (2017). "Kant and Hutcheson on Aesthetics and Teleology." In *Kant and the Scottish Enlightenment*, ed. by Elizabeth Robinson and Chris Surprenant, Milton Park.
Winegar, Reed (2021). "Kant's Antinomy of Taste and the Supersensible." In *The Court of Reason*. Akten des 13. Internationalen Kant-Kongresses (Oslo, 6. bis 9. August 2019), ed. by Camilla Serck-Hanssen and Beatrix Himmelmann, Berlin, Boston.

Paul Guyer
Response

a) Preliminaries

I am honored and gratified by these papers from such accomplished and now distinguished former students of mine. I was fortunate throughout my career to be able to work with exceptionally promising graduate students (and some memorable undergraduates as well). Of course the six represented in this collection are only a fraction of others who could equally well have been invited (some of whom have contributed to several other collections in my honor, for all of which I am grateful).[1] Although I could not have formulated this as a principle at the outset, as Julian Wuerth notes I never wanted students who felt obliged to agree with me and who would carry on some "research program" that I might be supposed to have. Rather, I enjoyed students who would challenge me to make my own work better, just as I thought that my role was to push my objections to their views as hard as I could to help them make their work as good as it could be. The contributors to this volume certainly challenge me on a number of issues. If I push back, it is in the hope I can use this occasion, even at this stage of my career, to further refine my views, as several of the writers suggest I should do.

The papers by Fred Rauscher, Lucas Thorpe, Julian Wuerth, Wiebke Deimling and Kate Moran raise questions about both the substantive and meta-ethical aspects of my interpretation of Kant's practical philosophy over the years, while Reed Winegar argues that Kant connected aesthetics (concerned with both the beautiful and the sublime) and teleology earlier than I have suggested in my account of the genesis of Kant's third *Critique*. My approach to Kant's theoretical philosophy remains in the background in these essays, although my critique of Kant's approach to the problem of freedom of the will based on my critique of his arguments for transcendental idealism itself is acknowledged in several of the papers. I will discuss the issues about my interpretation of Kant's practical philosophy first and then come to the question about the novelty of the third *Critique*, as is any case appropriate in view of the sequence of Kant's own major publications. The substantive issue that dominates the discussion of my approach to Kant's practical philosophy in the papers by Rauscher, Thorpe, and Wuerth is whether I have appropriatly identified humanity as its foundation, and if so appropriately interpreted Kant's concept of humanity, or whether its foundation is not better

---

1 See Moran 2018 and Filieri and Møller 2024.

understood as pure reason as such. The meta-ethical or methodological issue is whether a naturalistic approach to Kant's practical philosophy can save what is most valuable in it, as I have several times attempted to argue, or whether a "transcendental" or aprioristic interpretation of Kant's most fundamental premises in practical philosophy is both necessary and possible. Rauscher, for example, although his own approach to Kant's practical philosophy is naturalistic in certain respects, is insistent that only a transcendental interpretation of Kant's premises will do, and Wuerth emphasizes that the emergence of Kant's mature moral philosophy goes hand in hand with the hardening of his distinction between sensibility and understanding, which also points in the direction of an aprioristic foundation for it. Deimling is willing to travel further with me down the path of a more naturalistic approach drawing on Kant's anthropology, that is, his empirical psychology, although she and I might both locate Kant's naturalism in his view of the conditions for the realization of morality given the nature of human psychology rather than in his attempt to provide a secure foundation for practical philosophy. So there is not necessarily any tension between an aprioristic approach to the foundations of practical philosophy and a more naturalistic account of the conditions for the realization or implementation of the demands of morality. (A word on terminology: I will generally refer to Kant's "practical philosophy" rather than to his "moral philosophy," because some dispute whether Kant's doctrine of right is properly part of his moral philosophy, while no one disputes that it is properly part of his practical philosophy. That debate, over the so-called "independence" thesis, does not come up in these papers, and I will sidestep it here by just referring to Kant's "practical philosophy." However, since I do in fact firmly believe that Kant's moral philosophy is divided into two parts, the set of coercively enforceable duties comprising the doctrine of right and the set of non-coercively enforceable duties comprising the doctrine of virtue or ethics,[2] I also believe that in discussing Kant the term "ethics" should never be used as synonymous with "moral philosophy" — ethics is only one part of moral philosophy. However, the contemporary term "meta-ethics" for the discussion of the methodology of practical philosophy is well nigh unavoidable, so I do not attempt to proscribe it.)

---

[2] See Guyer 2005a, chapter 9, and Guyer 2016b.

b) Foundational and Meta-Ethical Issues

I begin with the papers by Rauscher, Thorpe, and Wuerth, which all address my approach to the foundations of Kant's practical philosophy and join together in pressing my interpretation of humanity as an end in itself as that foundation for a necessary clarification. Rauscher raises both questions, about the proper starting-point for Kant's practical philosophy and about the proper understanding of its method. He interprets me as interpreting Kant as starting from the premise of the intrinsic and unconditional value of *humanity*, understood as freedom of choice, the freedom of every human being to set her own ends whether in accordance with the demands of the moral law or not, but as recommending a naturalistic interpretation of this capacity rather than a transcendental (I think I would say here "transcendent") one. By contrast, he argues that Kant derives morality from pure *reason* as such, which can avoid any unfounded assumption about the existence of an absolute and intrinsic *value* (or "value realism"), and that reason must and can be understood as a non-naturalistic transcendental (here I might say "a priori") capacity — although one that can be attributed to us as beings in a really spatio-temporal world, not as things in ourselves, with libertarian free wills, in a noumenal realm. (This is Rauscher's own, partially naturalistic interpretation of Kant.) As he sums up, "Reason's practical application carries with it normativity since, as rational beings, we experience our rationality as a demand for rational consistency. This kind of transcendental ground does not require any non-natural ontology beyond a conception of reason itself having a special status as the ground of law independent of natural law."

Let me concede from the outset, and as applying to much in these papers, that we can often find textual support for competing interpretations of Kant — it might be heretical to say so in this journal, but while Kant was a profound philosopher, he was not always a very precise philosopher. In this case, room for competing interpretations is immediately created by Kant's explication of the "ground of a possible categorical imperative" in the *Groundwork for the Metaphysics of Morals*: first he says that "the human being *and in general every rational being exists* as an end in itself, *not merely as a means* to be used by this or that will at is discretion," and that *"rational beings* are called *persons* because their nature already marks them out as an end in itself,"[3] but then he says that the — grounding,

---

[3] GMS, AA 04: 428; my emphasis added by underlining. Translations from Kant's writings in practical philosophy are from Kant 1996a; from the *Critique of Pure Reason* from Kant 1998; and from the *Critique of the Power of Judgment* from Kant 2000.

thus most fundamental — formulation of the "practical imperative will therefore be the following: *So act that you use* **humanity**, *whether in your own person or that of an other, always at the same time as an end, never merely as a means.*"[4] So, as far as text is concerned, rational being or rationality vs. humanity? — take your pick. Nevertheless, I have several reservations about Rauscher's alternative to my approach.

First, for Kant reason is in the first instance *formal*, that is, needs to be applied to some content that it does not itself give (although, not in the first instance, it does, but problematically, create concepts of objects of its own, the ideas of reason, by adding the concept of the "unconditioned" to otherwise formal categories such as *subject* or *ground*). To take the most fundamental principle of reason, namely the principle of non-contradiction, this has to be applied to something, a concept or a proposition, to determine whether it is free of self-contradiction or not, or a pair of propositions, to determine whether they are mutually contradictory or not. This is why I impute to Kant the view, found early in some of the notes in his copy of *Observations on the Feeling of the Beautiful and Sublime* but also, I claim, close to the surface in the explication of the second formulation of the categorical imperative in the *Groundwork* from which I just quoted, that we have to apply the principle of non-contradiction to our knowledge of the fact that persons possess humanity including the ability to set their own ends, that is, not act in ways that imply the contradiction of this fact. In application to the fact of our humanity, the principle of non-contradiction yields this great result; by itself, it yields nothing. Or, identify reason with the demand for universal validity: if this is applied to the idea of agents who formulate and act upon maxims of action, thus construed as requiring the universalizability of any permissible maxim of action, then it yields a great result; if it is not applied to the idea of maxims adopted by agents, it yields nothing. Thus I might say that humanity without reason is blind, but reason without humanity is empty. At the very least, Rauscher and I need to meet on a middle ground. I will come back to this issue in my comments on the papers by Thorpe and Wuerth as well.

Second, but not unrelated to the point that I have just made, Kant himself obviously regards reason and will, or at least pure reason and pure will, as closely connected. This is evident in the "fact of reason" passage in the *Critique of Practical Reason*, when he asserts that "We can become aware of pure practical laws just as we [become] aware of pure theoretical principles, by attending to the necessity with which reason prescribes them to us [...] *The concept of a pure will*

---

4 GMS, AA 04: 29, my emphasis added in underlining. I will return to the issue about the foundational status of humanity for Kant in my comments on Thorpe's paper.

arises from the first, as consciousness of a pure understanding arises from the latter. That this is the true subordination of our concepts and that morality first discloses to us the concept of freedom [...] is clear [...]."[5] For Kant himself, possession of pure reason, pure practical reason only in the sense that it is pure reason applied to the case of action, goes hand in hand with possession of a pure will. They cannot be separated, and thus the threat of the transcendent, if that is what it is, cannot be avoided as easily as Rauscher proposes, by limiting the claim to pure reason alone; as a matter of Kant interpretation, if not of what we ourselves might believe, possession of a pure reason cannot be separated from possession of a pure will, and if the latter requires a dubious noumenal location, it is not clear that the former need not.

But, third, and again connected, there is the issue of the "Ulrich/Sidgwick" objection, i.e., the objection to the implication that we are only truly free when we are acting in accordance with the law of pure reason, that is, the moral law, thus not free, and therefore not imputable or responsible, when we act contrary to it. Rauscher says that he is happy to "bite the bullet" and accept the objection, because he does not want to defend Kant's transcendental idealist, noumenalist defense of libertarian freedom of the will, the ability to choose to act with or against the moral law no matter what one's (phenomenal) history seems to necessitate. I do not want to accept that defense either, but as a matter of Kant interpretation I do not think that one can have a "transcendental" conception of reason without a transcendent conception of freedom of the will. I think that this is clear in the second *Critique*, when Kant immediately illustrates what he means by a "pure will" with the example of the man who is free not to bear false witness to another to his prince even on pain of his own death, *although he does not know whether or not he will obey the moral law or his prince* — that he does not know which he will do assumes precisely that he is free to do either. That is Kant's view of freedom, and of the condition for responsibility; and if one is not going to buy it, then one owes an alternative account of the condition for responsibility. Of course Rauscher could not have provided his alternative account of it here, but he has to acknowledge the debt.

Finally, what Kant thought aside, I think that Rauscher has to be right that we can have a transcendental account of the purity of reason without accepting a transcendent account of the powers of a noumenal self. Even the most committed naturalist (and materialist), who believes that all human capacities must be at least in principle explicable as the product of carbon-based molecules in electrochemical motion, must also admit that we humans are capable of logic and math-

---

5 KpV, AA 05: 30; my emphasis added by underlining.

ematics, for example formulating, understanding, and applying the principle of non-contradiction, Aristotelian syllogistic or the method of natural deduction, arithmetic, and so on. You do not have to be a Kantian to agree that we have some forms of a priori cognition; naturalists could not explain how we can even argue about naturalism itself unless they are willing to acknowledge that we somehow recognize the validity of the principle of non-contradiction, of the forms of permissible, truth-preserving inference, and so on. I would not ask Rauscher to explain how this is possible without transcendental idealism, because I am sure that I cannot explain it. But it does cry out for explanation.

Turning to the papers by Lucas Thorpe and Julian Wuerth, let me begin by emphasizing the importance of my meeting Rauscher halfway, that is, recognizing the importance of *both* freedom and reason in Kant's concept of humanity. Thorpe distinguishes between autonomy, "understood as the capacity for sovereignty," as the "source of the dignity of humanity," on the one hand, and "freedom understood as the capacity to set ends" as, on my account, "the ultimate value for Kant." Let me identify Thorpe's concept of autonomy, for the moment, with reason, in particular pure practical reason, although in the end my concept of pure practical reason and his of autonomy are not quite identical. But detail aside, his distinction between the source of dignity and the ultimate value — or I might say end — in Kant's practical philosophy may suggest the way for me to meet Rauscher halfway. This goes for Wuerth as well, whose first point is that my interpretation of Kant's conception of humanity must be expanded beyond freedom, that is, the capacity to set our own ends, to include our capacity for morality or for a good will, because it is the latter that gives us our dignity and thus our entitlement to moral regard. Let me make this point by stepping back for a moment from the particular terms introduced by Rauscher, Thorpe, and Wuerth. In general, interpretations of Kant's concept of humanity have fallen into three camps: that of Richard Dean, which identified humanity with actually being moral, or realizing a good will;[6] that exemplified by Henry Allison, which identified humanity with the *capacity* to be moral;[7] and that identified with Allen Wood[8] and myself, which has identified humanity with the freedom of humans to set their own ends (on this account humanity is not identical with all of the prototypical capacities of biologically human beings, but with the specific capacity to set ends that could be exemplified by other sorts of rational agents as well, if there are any, although if there are any such other sorts of beings then this same capacity would presumably go

---

6 See Dean 2006, and for some refinement Dean 2021.
7 See Allison 2011, 215–218.
8 See Wood 1999, e.g., 119, and Wood 2008, e.g., 91.

by a different name in their cases, reflecting their identity as in our case it reflects ours by being called "humanity"). Dean's approach has generally been rejected on the ground that in Kant's view even those who themselves violate the moral law, thus do not have a good will, are owed moral regard from the rest of us, which is to say that we must continue to treat humanity in their person as an end and not merely as a means even if they themselves have not treated their own humanity or that of others as such an end. The second position, that by humanity Kant means the *capacity* of human beings to be moral (and *mutatis mutandis* for any other rational beings there might be), has one strong piece of evidence in its favor, namely Kant's statement that it is "morality, and humanity *insofar as it is capable of morality*, [...] which alone has dignity."[9] But it also has the problem that it leaves unspecified *what it is to be moral*, or what the *content* of treating persons with dignity is supposed to be: it cannot be enough to say just that it is moral to treat persons as capable of morality, if we do not know anything further about what morality requires. The interpretation of humanity as the capacity, or freedom, of human beings to set their own ends, gives content to the idea of morality: to treat humanity as an end and never merely as a means then means to treat the capacity to set one's own ends, *both* in one's own case *and* in that of every other person, as itself an end and not merely as a means, thus, whatever anyone's particular ends might be, to adopt such ends only when they are compatible with the (greatest possible) freedom of oneself *and everyone else* who might be affected by one's own actions, and further to make promoting or expanding the freedom of all itself a positive end, indeed, an end to be effected. (Thus both perfect and imperfect duties can be derived from this idea.)[10] It can then be argued, however, that it is the capacity for morality, or to set one's ends in the morally permissible and mandatory way, that gives humans their dignity, or entitles them to moral regard, while it is their freedom to set their own ends that gives content to morality, that is, to what morality demands for them in virtue of their dignity. It could also be argued that this is the way to make sense of Kant's statement that it is their capacity for morality that gives persons their dignity and their entitlement to moral regard together with his definition of humanity as simply "the capacity to set oneself an

---

9 GMS, AA 04: 435; my emphasis is added by underlining. Wuerth also cites this passage.
10 Wood has emphasized Kant's characterization of humanity as a "self-sufficient end" (*selbständiger Zweck*) rather than an "end to be effected" (*zu bewirkender Zweck*); Wood 1999, 115, referring to GMS, AA 04: 437. It is certainly true that Kant never suggests that we have a moral obligation to bring rational or human beings into existence, the way we might bring other sorts of ends into existence, but humanity as the capacity to set ends certainly can be preserved and promoted (expanded) by our efforts, and in that sense is an end "to be effected." Otherwise Kant's eventual catalogue of human duties in the *Metaphysics of Morals* would make no sense.

end — *any end whatsoever.*"¹¹ Thus I can agree with Wuerth that it is the "capacity, specifically, for a good will that comprises the worth of humanity" without giving up my interpretation that without the conception of humanity as the capacity to set our own ends morality would be empty. To be sure, being able to set an end at all, as contrasted to merely having a desire, involves reason, but perhaps only the empirical use of practical reason, manifested in technical imperatives and counsels of prudence, while the capacity for morality requires also the use of pure practical reason: the capacity for morality in rational *agents* is the capacity to set particular ends, any particular ends whatever, but in accordance with the demands of morality that emanate from pure practical reason — from our autonomy, if you will. Kant's full conception of humanity must include both empirical and pure uses of practical reason, that is, practical uses of reason as such.

These are the general terms in which I think that I can meet both Rauscher, Thorpe, and Wuerth halfway. Thorpe is also correct to observe that "Kant is systematically ambiguous in the way in which he uses the word 'humanity'." For while in the *Groundwork* Kant's usage of the term at the very least includes the capacity for morality, in *Religion within the Boundaries of Mere Reason* Kant distinguishes between humanity and personality, where it is the latter rather than the former that seems to be identified with the capacity for morality: "personality is the susceptibility to respect for the moral law *as of itself a sufficient incentive to the power of choice* [*Willkühr*]"; by contrast, the "predispositions to humanity can be brought under the general title of a self-love which is physical and yet *involves comparison* (for which reason is required); that is, only in comparison with others does one judge oneself happy or unhappy."¹² Here Kant does not explicitly identify humanity with the capacity to set oneself an end, but, first, note that he speaks of *predispositions* to humanity in the plural, so he is not simply reducing it to the tendency to compare ourselves and our condition to others, and, second, that self-love does involve setting ends, namely aiming at this or that for oneself with the aim of gratification but with possible disregard for morality. As Thorpe points out, Kant sometimes uses a term for both a genus and one of its species, as when he uses "reason" generically to subtend both understanding and reason more narrowly construed. The same could occur here, as when he sometimes uses "humanity" generically to subtend both humanity narrowly understood, as the ability to set oneself an end, and personality, as the ability to make the moral law a sufficient incentive and governing constraint for one's adoption of any particular end (through the adoption of a maxim). Thus humanity understood in its generic sense

---

11 MS, TL, Introduction, section VIII.1, AA 06: 692.
12 RGV, Part One, AA 06: 27. Translation from Kant 1996b.

would include both the capacity to set ends and the capacity to be moral, although the latter should govern the former. But just as the cognitive faculties have their "lower" and "higher" forms, that is, their empirical and pure forms, so too would humanity: we *can* set our ends in accordance with pure practical reason, i.e., morality, but can also do so in accordance with merely empirical practical reason, i.e., self-love, and that prudently or imprudently. Indeed, it is in precisely that possibility of choosing either way that our freedom of will (here *Willkühr*) consists, contrary to the view of freedom that Rauscher wants to promote. And, if one wants to adopt the view that it is in our capacity to be moral that our dignity consists or is grounded, one could explicate that by saying that it is in our capacity to choose to set our particular ends in accordance with the demands of morality *when it is morally imperative that we choose that way but our nature does not metaphysically necessitate that we do so* that our dignity really lies: our dignity lies precisely in the fact that we can *freely* choose to be moral: "there is indeed no sublimity" "in the person who fulfills all his duties" simply "insofar as he is *subject* to the moral law, but there certainly is insofar as he is at the same time *lawgiving* with respect to it and only for that reason subject to it."[13]

In these ways, then, I welcome Thorpe's contribution. But there are two points on which I cannot follow him. First, I cannot follow him in adopting Wilfrid Sellars's conception of the moral will as a "we-intention," thus, "to Guyerize Sellars," in the explication of the moral will as "We-intend that it be the case that the freedom **of each of us** (individually) be promoted." I think that this gets the *object* of the moral will right, as a matter both of Kant interpretation and of fact, but not the *subject* of the moral will. That is, I think that "that the freedom **of each us**" be promoted — and preserved, indeed preserved before being promoted; that is the lexical priority of perfect over imperfect duty — is exactly what treating humanity both in our own person and that of every other always as an end and never merely as a means requires — it is in this sense that humanity *is* an "end to be effected — but that to adopt this fundamental principle is a duty incumbent *on each of us*, which *each of us* must strive to fulfill, but which none of us can do for any other. We can encourage each other in various ways to fulfill our individual duty — that is what moral education and the "ethico-civil state" or "ethical community" are for[14] — but ultimately we must each perfect our own moral capacity. No one else can do that for us, which is why the happiness of others but not their perfection is an end that is also a duty. This is why Kant says, at his strictest, that "we have a duty, but only a negative one, to promote" the *"moral well-being"* of

---

13   GMS, AA 04: 440.
14   RGV, Part Three, AA 06: 95–96.

others, "to refrain from doing anything that, considering the nature of a human being, could tempt [another] to do something for which his conscience could afterwards pain him."[15] There is no such thing as a collective subject in the Kantian universe (and in real life, too, I would contend, the obligations of collectives always have to be cashed out as obligations of individuals, however the effort of any individual might only contribute a small piece of a collective goal. Indeed, to think anything else risks shunting off the obligations of individuals to some metaphysically dubious collective agent. I am aware that the possibility of collective agency and responsibility is a big issue in contemporary moral and political philosophy, but here I will just be dogmatic about it.

This leads to my other concern with Thorpe's position, namely my objection to any suggestion that we should consider (what I prefer to translate as) the empire of ends (*Reich der Zwecke*), as more fundamental in the argument of the *Groundwork* than the concept of humanity. To be sure, the empire of ends *is* a "plausible candidate" for the "universally valid end" of morality. But this is because such an empire, namely "a whole both of rational beings as ends in themselves and of the ends of his own that each may set himself,"[16] is what would directly *result* if *each* individual agent were to treat the humanity in *every* agent — as including the capacity to set his or her own ends — as an end and never merely as a means. So I would say that the humanity in each person is the *immediate* object of the good will and the empire of ends the *proximate* object. Or, the concept of humanity, now as including the capacity for morality, explains why every person is due moral regard from, or is an object of moral obligation for, every person, and the concept of the empire of ends expresses what would result if such moral regard were actually forthcoming. As Kant himself puts it, "an empire of ends […] is possible in accordance with the above principles,"[17] that is, with the preceding formulae of universal law and of humanity, where however the latter is the "ground of the possibility of a categorical imperative" and includes the requirement of universality when it says that humanity in one's own person *and that of every other* is to be treated as an end and never merely as a means. Kant puts the same point in another way in his summary of the exposition of the three (main) formulae of the categorical imperative, when he says that every maxim must have a "form," namely universality (universalizability), a "matter," namely that it must regard every rational being "as an end by its nature and hence as an end in itself," and *then* a "complete determination," namely it must specify a condition for and con-

---

15 MS, TL, Introduction, section VIII.2, AA 06: 394.
16 GMS, AA 04: 433.
17 GMS, AA 04: 433.

tribution to the realization of an empire of ends.[18] This makes it clear that the status of humanity as an end in itself is argumentatively antecedent to the idea of the empire of ends, and that the status of the latter as the complete object of morality follows from the former.

The idea of a complete object of morality should lead us to discussion of Kate Moran's discussion of the highest good. But before I turn to that, let me comment on the second main point of Wuerth's contribution. As I already mentioned, Wuerth argues that Kant's mature practical philosophy emerges along with his emphasis on the distinction between sensibility and understanding, both taking their decisive turn around 1769–70, and that the characteristic methodology of Kant's mature moral philosophy is therefore the "Elimination of Sensibility Procedure," that is, the elimination of any possible sensible and empirical basis for a universally valid fundamental principle of morality, leaving only the possibility of a formal principle and rational ground for it. The thought is that a formal principle, stripped of all empirical content, must lead to the Formula of Universal Law, that is, of course, the requirement that morally permissible maxims of action must be universalizable without contradiction, and that this principle, validated by pure reason itself, does not need the "matter" of humanity for its validation. Now, there can be no doubt that this captures how Kant at least begins the derivation of the categorical imperative (always to be distinguished from the fundamental principle of morality, valid for all rational beings, as the form in which this principle presents itself to us imperfectly rational human beings)[19] in the *Groundwork*,[20] and that it is his whole argument for the categorical imperative in the *Critique of Practical Reason*.[21] However, I emphasize three textual reasons why the "Elimination of Sensibility Procedure," important as it clearly is to Kant, cannot be the whole of his argument for his understanding of the fundamental principle of morality. First, in the Doctrine of Method of the *Critique of Pure Reason*, thus quite late in the book, but at a point at which he is reflecting upon his methodology throughout the work, on "the discipline of pure reason in regard to its proofs," he says that in transcendental philosophy arguments cannot be just "apagogic" but must also be "ostensive," which I take to mean that they cannot be just arguments by elimination, but must ultimately adduce some "direct," positive ground for their conclusion.[22] I take it that in his practical philosophy Kant derives the first

---

18 GMS, AA 04: 436.
19 See GMS, AA 04: 412.
20 See GMS, both AA 04: 401f and 421.
21 See KpV, Theorem III, AA 05: 27.
22 KrV, A 789/B 817.

formulation of the categorical imperative (FUL) by an apagogic argument, and in the *Critique of Practical Reason*, which is primarily concerned with freedom of the will and the highest good rather than with the very foundation of practical philosophy, he is content to leave it at that, but that in the *Groundwork*, which as the title suggests is fundamentally concerned with the foundation of practical philosophy, he does mean to proceed beyond an apagogic argument to an ostensive one — and that it is humanity as an end in itself which is supposed to be the direct ground for that which has been indirectly derived by an argument by elimination. Second, in the Feyerabend lectures on natural right, given in the summer of 1784, thus at the very time he was writing the *Groundwork*, Kant is recorded as having said that "If rational beings are capable of being ends in themselves it cannot be because they have reason but because they have freedom. Reason is merely a means."[23] This is certainly compatible with the interpretation that it is humanity, as the freedom to set one's own ends, which is the matter of morality, and that the requirement of universalizability, as the product of pure reason rather than sensibility, is only the means to ensure that this end is realized for everyone. Finally, in the *Groundwork* itself, Kant plainly says that there needs to be a "ground of a possible categorical imperative," and that this must be something that is an end in itself; rational being, in our case in the form of our humanity, is the candidate for this.[24] Kant surely regards the argument by elimination that has yielded the formal constraint of universalizability on maxims as incomplete without the matter of humanity, as he also makes clear in his own summary of the three formulae of the categorical imperative.[25]

To be sure, all this leaves the question of how Kant intends to establish that humanity *is* the sole end in itself that could ground the categorical imperative. Wuerth's emphasis on the significance of Kant's distinction between sensibility and understanding (or intellect or reason more generally) makes it clear that it cannot be a mere feeling, even a feeling on behalf of freedom, as Kant might have contemplated before 1769 (though we will come back to the question of a "passion for freedom" in the discussion of Deimling's paper below). In Section II of the *Groundwork*, Kant suggests what I have elsewhere called "normative essentialism," that our nature simply "marks us out" as ends in ourselves. In the crucial argument of Section III, he seems to suggest that we can know that as we are in ourselves we are spontaneous and free, which would open the way for an argument that we cannot act in a way that denies this without self-contradiction. In

---

23 V-NR/Feyerabend, AA 27: 1321, translation from Kant 2016.
24 GMS, AA 04: 428.
25 GMS, AA 04: 431.

the *Critique of Practical Reason*, he claims that our consciousness of the necessity of the moral law also reveals the purity of our will, thus of our freedom to us, thus that the former is the *ratio cognoscendi* of our freedom but freedom the *ratio essendi* of morality, which would be another way of saying that it is our freedom that is the ground of and reason for the necessity of morality. But all of these are just hints at an argument that we might have to conclude Kant never fully developed. We are certainly not going to fully develop it here.

Instead, we can now turn back to the question of the complete object of morality, or the highest good. This is the topic of Kate Moran's paper.

c) The Complete Object of Morality

Moran accepts the distinction that I have made between individualistic and collectivist strands in Kant's conception of the highest good (as part of my argument that the latter becomes more prominent as Kant's thought develops over the three *Critiques* and beyond, while the postulate of personal immortality which Kant insists is a necessary condition for rational belief in the realizability of the former fades).[26] She calls the first conception a composite one, combining morality's demand for individual virtue with a natural desire for one's own happiness, while the latter, the collectivist conception, is a unitary conception of the highest good: happiness is not introduced as a separate, natural end, rather the happiness of all is what would result from the virtue or good will of all, precisely because morality demands that each do her part in promoting the ends of all, and happiness is simply what follows from (or is equivalent) to the satisfaction of ends, thus the happiness of all is what follows from the promotion of the ends of all. This raises the question whether there is any difference between the collectivist conception of the highest good and the idea of the empire of ends, on which my own position is, not really: the fullest possible promotion of the ends of all that would be realized in an empire of ends would be or produce the greatest happiness that is possible in the world. Or, the collective highest good would be the result of the historical realization of a genuine empire of ends. This is a "secular" conception of the highest good, as Andrews Reath called it long ago,[27] insofar as it proposes the eventual realization of the empire of ends in the course of the natural history of the human species without postulating individual immortality, but, as Moran

---

26 See Guyer 2020a, chapter 4.
27 See Reath 1988.

correctly notes, for Kant it is by no means entirely secular, because it still postulates, in Kant's terms, an author of the laws of nature that are consistent with the moral law, or, as a contemporary like Adam Smith would have put it, Providence. About this conception of the highest good, Moran rightly asks whether we really need positive grounds for belief in its possibility, or rather, given the moral importance of the goal, as the complete object of morality, whether reason *not* to believe in the *im*possibility of realizing the goal would not be sufficient to make our efforts toward realizing it rational.[28]

According to Moran, however, in the composite individualistic conception of the highest good, the relation between the virtue or morality of the individual agent and her happiness is a "conditioning" relation: her morality is a condition of the individual's ultimate happiness, but her happiness cannot be considered to be *caused* by her own morality — for one thing, as Kant makes plain in the *Critique of Pure Reason*, in the actual natural world the happiness of even the most virtuous person depends on the cooperation of others, which is by no means always forthcoming. It is thus this conception of the highest good which requires the postulation of both the existence of God and of personal immortality to make possible and actual the individual happiness that individual morality warrants, as Kant argued in the first two *Critiques*. There can be no doubt that Kant believed all of this. The question is how does individual happiness come to be of any moral significance at all: it is clear enough why individual morality should be a necessary condition for happiness, *as for anything else*, but why should morality care enough about individual happiness for *that* to be what individual morality is a condition for? Moran quotes the well-known passage from the beginning of the Dialectic of Pure Practical Reason in which Kant suggests that it would be a failure in the eye of "impartial reason" if individual happiness were not, eventually and ultimately, accompanied by individual happiness.[29] But why should impartial reason care about this? However, an answer to the question why morality should care about the *collectivist* highest good can be found, when Kant comes to work out the details of his metaphysics of morals, in the duty to promote the happiness of others as the second end that is also a duty: if everyone were to promote the happiness of everyone else, then of course the happiness of everyone would be promoted even if no one were promoting their own happiness in the name of morality. And perhaps the *first* end that is also a duty, namely the duty of self-perfection, can help bring *individual* happiness under the aegis of morality after all. For the duty of self-perfection includes the duty to perfect one's *moral* capaci-

---

28 The line that I took in Guyer 2000, chapter 10.
29 KpV, AA 05: 110.

ties — which one might have thought is not different from the duty to be moral in general — but also the duty to perfect one's *natural* capacities, one's potential skills and talents of body, spirit, and mind, and the perfection of these are precisely what would allow one to set realizable ends for oneself, and thereby to bring about one's own happiness (as well as to successfully promote the happiness of others). Perhaps there is something of a causal connection between the development of one's own virtue and the realization of one's own happiness after all, although to be sure Kant did not want that causal connection to be so strong that God and immortality were no longer necessary to complete the connection between individual morality and happiness. This is an argument that would need to be worked out.

d) Moral Anthropology

Finally I turn to aspects of Kant's moral anthropology, that is, what it is for us humans to try to satisfy the demands of morality under the empirical circumstances of our existence.[30] Wiebke Deimling takes up the idea of a "passion for reason" that I introduced in my Presidential Address for the Eastern Division of the American Philosophical Association.[31] Drawing on a comparison with Hume's view that reason can determine means but that ends are determined only by passion, I argued there that even if Kant can succeed in deriving the moral law as the form of pure practical reason, he would still need to posit something like a fundamental desire to be rational, or choice to be rational, in order to explain the normative force of the idea of being rational itself. Perhaps one way to explicate the difference between Kant's arguments in the *Groundwork* and the *Critique of Practical Reason* would be to say that while Kant tries to sidestep the need for such an affective element in Section III of the former by insisting that (at the noumenal level) we are essentially rational (this is of course what opens him up to the Ulrich objection), in the "fact of reason" passage of the latter work he recognizes that we have a choice whether to be rational or not, that is, are not automatically rational, thus may need to have some sort of desire to be rational. Of course, Kant could not countenance a literal "passion for reason," since he defines passion as an affective state that blocks the exercise of reason, so a passion for reason can be at best an analogue of a Kantian passion strictly so called. However, as I noted

---

30 See MS, Introduction, AA 06: 216–217.
31 Originally 2011, in Guyer 2016, chapter 12.

in that address, in his anthropology Kant does recognize a passion for *freedom*, namely *one's own freedom*, beginning in infancy, and since, on my account, the preservation and promotion of freedom, but the maximal compatible freedom of *all*, is in fact what pure practical reason requires of us, this passion for one's own freedom can be co-opted for the sake of morality by being transformed by reason into a quasi-passion for the freedom of all — insofar as reason is involved in this transformation, to be sure, the result will not literally be a passion. This is part of moral anthropology: how humans can become moral in the empirical world, given their nature. Deimling develops this aspect of Kant's moral anthropology in more detail than I did, explaining how, in Kant's view, our passions for honor, power, and possession can be redirected and refined to facilitate the development of our rational agency. She also brings Rousseau into the story. Deimling's account is a valuable supplement to my treatment of the "aesthetic preconditions of the mind's susceptibility to the concept of duty," where Kant asserts that we have an indirect duty to "cultivate" and "strengthen" conscience and several varieties of moral feeling without much elaboration.[32] Deimling's account of Kant's moral anthropology is also important because it helps connect Kant's foundational writings in moral philosophy to his philosophy of history, as expressed in such works as the "Idea for a Universal History," "The Conjectural Beginning of Human History," and *Toward Perpetual Peace*, as well as to his characterization of humanity in the *Religion*: the natural tendencies to comparison and competition, at the individual and the national level, like the passions that Deimling describes, are the mechanisms that nature affords us that we *can* use to drive moral progress. I say "*can* use," because, in spite of the suggestion otherwise in *Perpetual Peace*, it would be contrary to Kant's final conception of human to think that any natural mechanism *guarantees* moral progress — that would take the decision to be moral, or not, out of our own hands, where on Kant's view it is firmly lodged.

Last but not least, I come to the contribution by Reed Winegar. Prior to the publication of the *Critique of the Power of Judgment*, Kant discussed aesthetics chiefly in his lectures on anthropology, and more briefly in the lectures on metaphysics, in both cases because Baumgarten included a brief account of his aesthetics in the chapter on empirical psychology in his *Metaphysica*, the whole of which was the text for Kant's metaphysics lectures while that chapter was his text for the anthropology lectures. Kant did not explicitly label his account of the relations of his mature aesthetics and teleology to morality as part of his moral anthropology. However, we might regard the connections that Kant tries to establish between the

---

[32] See MS, TL, Introduction, section XIII, AA 06: 399–402; my 2010 paper on moral feelings in the *Metaphysics of Morals* is reprinted as Guyer 2016a, chapter 14.

several forms of aesthetic experience as well as our teleological view of nature, on the one hand, and the development of our morality, on the other, as part of his moral anthropology, because it is clear that these links are intended to be valid for human beings in particular, not for rational beings in general — other rational beings might not have feelings at all, thus no aesthetic experience, thus neither need nor be able to use aesthetic experience to support their morality (God would be a case in point), and similarly the necessity of teleological judgment seems to be a human peculiarity, while other rational beings might be capable of a fully mechanical comprehension of nature

I argued in a 2003 paper (in a volume of papers on Kant's anthropology)[33] that it was Kant's late recognition that both aesthetic and teleological judgment could be supportive of or conducive to our moral development that prompted him to combine the "critique of taste" that he had long envisioned with teleology in a way that he had previously not done. Winegar argues that Kant had written of both beauty and sublimity in moral contexts long before that time in 1787 when according to me he first conceived of a unified third *Critique*, and that Kant's early references to the sublime anticipate more of his account in that third *Critique* than I allow. Thus my account needs to be refined. Of course Kant referred to both the beautiful and the sublime in the 1764 *Observations*, but Winegar discusses the 1755 *Universal Natural History and Theory of the Heavens* and the 1763 *The Only Possible Basis for a Demonstration of the Existence of God*, Kant's most extensive pre-critical treatment of teleology before the critical treatment of it in the third *Critique* (where teleological judgment is held to be a necessity for us human beings but to be "heautonomous," that is, prescriptive for us but not prescriptive for our constitutive of nature itself — in other words, Kant's mature teleology is part of his anthropology).[34] Indeed, in these works Kant does often describe the order that we find in nature, including even geometric relations, as beautiful, suggesting, as Winegar argues, that "natural beauty is morally significant, given that it leads to a conviction in God's existence that both promotes virtuous behavior and promises future happiness." And Kant also argues in these early works that nature in its magnitude, like that "of a planetary system in which the earth is as a grain of sand" is astonishing and sublime. But while Winegar acknowledges that "the line between the beautiful and the sublime is not always sharp in Kant's early writings," I would go further, and counter that Kant's uses of the concepts of the beautiful and the sublime are entirely conventional, hinting at nothing of the original analyses or explications of both the beautiful and the sublime that he would de-

---

33 Reprinted as Guyer 2005b, chapter 7.
34 See Guyer 2020b.

velop in his mature work, and that his suggestion of the moral significance of the aesthetic dimensions of nature, as evidence of God's benevolence, is also quite conventional (for example, see the final chapter of Francis Hutcheson's 1725 treatise "Concerning Beauty, Order, Etc.").[35] This may well be a refinement of my earlier argument, but I would contend that there is no sign in Kant's early writings of his understanding of the experiences of both the beautiful and the sublime as experiences of *our own freedom*, and indirectly or directly morally significant for that reason, nor of his later argument that teleological judgment can point the way to a conception of the "ultimate end" of *nature* as the development of human *discipline* which however must be complemented with a recognition of the (moral) exercise of human *freedom* as the (supersensible) "final end" of nature. I will not rehearse all the details of these analyses here, which I have discussed many times before;[36] suffice it to say that Kant analyzes the experience of beauty as an experience of the free play of our own imagination (within the confines of the "lawfulness" demanded by the understanding), which allows the beautiful to serve as a symbol of the morally good and the experience of beauty to prepare the way for our own disinterested morality; that he analyzes the experience of the sublime in nature as at bottom an experience of the scope of our own pure reason and of the power of reason in its practical use to overcome the threats and blandishments of mere nature, an experience that prepares us to meet the demands of morality even when those are contrary to our personal interests; and that our teleological judgment beginning with the judgment of particular organisms but leading to the judgment of nature as a whole as a purposive system leads us to the recognition that only the realization of our own freedom in morality can give a point to the very existence of nature. I do not think that any of this is to be found in Kant's early writings. Indeed, I would suggest that Kant's *rejection* of the thought that regular relations in geometry, admirable as they might be, can trigger the *free play* that is essential to the experience of beauty is in fact a rejection of the earlier, conventional conception of beauty that he had allowed in favor of the new conception that he had reached in the third *Critique*.[37] Only once Kant had come to understand aesthetic experiences as experiences of freedom in their several ways, morality itself as essentially about the preservation and promotion of freedom, and even a teleological view of nature itself as culminating in a recognition of our own moral exercise of freedom as the final end of nature, could he have linked these topics in the way that he did in the *Critique of the Power of Judgment*.

---

35 See Hutcheson 2008, Treatise I, section VIII.
36 See Guyer 2005a, chapter 12, and Guyer 2005c.
37 See KU, "General remark on the first section of the Analytic" following § 22, AA 05: 241.

These essays have indeed pressed me to refine my views in several ways. I hope that readers of *Kant-Studien* have found them as enjoyable and stimulating as I did.

References

Allison, Henry E. (2011). *Kant's* Groundwork for the Metaphysics of Morals: *A Commentary*. Oxford: Oxford University Press.
Dean, Richard (2006). *The Value of Humanity in Kant's Moral Theory*. Oxford: Oxford University Press.
Filieri, Luigi and Sofie Møller, editors (2024). *Kant on Freedom and Human Nature*. London: Routledge.
Guyer, Paul (2000). *Kant on Freedom, Law, and Happiness*. Cambridge: Cambridge University Press.
Guyer, Paul (2005a). *Kant's System of Nature and Freedom: Selected Essays*. Oxford: Clarendon Press.
Guyer, Paul (2005b). *Values of Beauty: Historical Essays in Aesthetics*. Cambridge: Cambridge University Press.
Guyer, Paul (2005c). "The Difficulty of the Sublime." In C. Madelein, J. Pieters, and B. Vandenabeele, eds., *Histories of the Sublime*. Brussels: Koninklijke Vlaamse Academie van België voor Wetenschapen en Kunsten, 33–43.
Guyer, Paul (2016a). *Virtues of Freedom: Selected Essays on Kant*. Oxford: Oxford University Press.
Guyer, Paul (2016b). "The Twofold Morality of Kantian *Recht*." *Kant-Studien* 107, 34–63.
Guyer, Paul (2020a). *Reason and Experience in Mendelssohn and Kant*. Oxford: Oxford University Press.
Guyer, Paul (2020b). "'The Revised Method of Physico-Theology': Kant's Reformed Teleology." In Jeffrey McDonough, ed. *Teleology: Oxford Philosophical Concepts*. Oxford: Oxford University Press, 186–218.
Hutcheson, Francis (2008). *An Inquiry into the Original of Our Ideas of Beauty and Virtue*. Edited by Wolfgang Leidhold. Revised edition. Indianapolis: Liberty Fund.
Kant, Immanuel (1996a). *Practical Philosophy*. Edited and translated by Mary J. Gregor. Cambridge: Cambridge University Press.
Kant, Immanuel (1996b). *Religion and Rational Theology*. Edited and translated by Allen W. Wood and George di Giovanni. Cambridge: Cambridge University Press.
Kant, Immanuel (1998). *Critique of Pure Reason*. Edited and translated by Paul Guyer and Allen W. Wood. Cambridge: Cambridge University Press.
Kant, Immanuel (2000). *Critique of the Power of Judgment*. Edited by Paul Guyer, translated by Paul Guyer and Eric Matthews. Cambridge: Cambridge University Press.
Kant, Immanuel (2016). *Lectures and Drafts on Political Philosophy*. Edited by Frederick Rauscher, translated by Frederick Rauscher and Kenneth R. Westphal. Cambridge: Cambridge University Press.
Moran, Kate A., editor (2018). *Kant on Freedom and Spontaneity*. Cambridge: Cambridge University Press.
Reath, Andrews (1988). "Two Conceptions of the Highest Good in Kant." *Journal of the History of Philosophy* 26, 593–619.
Wood, Allen (1999). *Kant's Ethical Thought*. Cambridge: Cambridge University Press.
Wood, Allen (2008). *Kantian Ethics*. Cambridge: Cambridge University Press.

Notes on Authors

Wiebke Deimling is an associate professor of philosophy at Clark University. She works on Kant, early modern European philosophy, and the philosophy of art. Most of her research focuses on questions about the emotions. She has published various articles, including "Kant's Pragmatic Concept of Emotions" and "Kant's Theory of Tragedy".

Paul Guyer is the Jonathan Nelson Professor emeritus of Humanities and Philosophy at Brown University. He is the author, editor, and/or translator of more than thirty books, many on the philosophy of Kant. He was General Co-Editor of the Cambridge Edition of Immanuel Kant (1986–2016), and co-translator of the first and third *Critiques* and Kant's notes and fragments. His recent books include *Kant on the Rationality of Morality* (2019), *Reason and Experience in Mendelssohn and Kant* (2020), *A Philosopher Looks at Architecture* (2021), *Idealism in Modern Philosophy* (2023, with Rolf-Peter Horstmann), and *Kant's Impact on Moral Philosophy* (2024). He is a Fellow of the American Academy of Arts and Sciences and a Corresponding Member of the Academy of Athens.

Kate Moran is an associate professor of philosophy at Brandeis University in Massachusetts, USA. Recent and forthcoming books include *Kant's Ethics* (2022), and *A Philosopher Looks at Clothes* (forth.). Together with Martin Brecher, she is preparing an updated translation of Kant's *Doctrine of Right* as a German-English edition.

Frederick Rauscher is Professor of Philosophy at Michigan State University. His work includes the book *Naturalism and Realism in Kant's Ethics*, editing and co-translating Kant's *Lectures and Drafts on Political Philosophy*, and numerous papers on Kant's metaethics, political philosophy, and other topics, including "Kant's Moral Anti-Realism" and "Death and the Limits to State Coercive Power".

Lucas Thorpe is associate professor of philosophy and cognitive science at Boğaziçi University in Istanbul. He is the author of *The Kant Dictionary* (Bloomsbury) and co-editor of *Kant and the Concept of Community* (North American Kant Society Studies in Philosophy) and numerous articles on Kant, including "Kant, Guyer and Tomasello on the Capacity to Recognize the Humanity of Others", "Is Kant's Realm of Ends a Unum per Se? Aquinas, Suárez, Leibniz and Kant on Composition", and "What is the Point of Studying Ethics According to Kant?".

Reed Winegar is associate professor of philosophy at Fordham University. He co-edited the volume *Infinity in Early Modern Philosophy* (Springer) and has published papers on Kant in various journals, including *Archiv für Geschichte der Philosophie*, *British Journal for the History of Philosophy*, *European Journal of Philosophy*, *Hegel Bulletin*, *Journal of the History of Philosophy*, and *Kantian Review*. In 2015–16 he was a VolkswagenStiftung/Mellon Fellow at the Freie Universität Berlin and in 2018 a guest professor at the Humboldt-Universität zu Berlin.

Julian Wuerth is Associate Professor of Philosophy at Vanderbilt University. He is the author of *Kant on Mind, Action, and Ethics* (Oxford University Press, 2014), and he also edited *The Cambridge Kant Lexicon* (Cambridge University Press, 2021) and co-edited *Perfecting Virtue: New Essay on Kantian Ethics and Virtue Ethics* (Cambridge University Press, 2011). He is currently writing a book for Routledge Press, *Kant's Questions: What Should I Do?*

www.ingramcontent.com/pod-product-compliance
Lightning Source LLC
Chambersburg PA
CBHW061942220426
43662CB00012B/2001